The Light of
Ten Thousand Suns

A FULL CIRCLE BOOK

The Light of
Ten Thousand Suns

Swami Veda Bharati

FULL
CIRCLE

THE LIGHT OF TEN THOUSAND SUNS
Copyright © Swami Veda Bharati also known as Usharbudh Arya

First Indian Paperback Edition, 2001
First Reprint, March, 2009
ISBN 81-7621-049-8

Published by

FULL CIRCLE *PUBLISHING*
J-40, Jorbagh Lane, New Delhi-110003
Tel: 24620063, 24621011 • Fax: 24645795
E-mail: fullcircle@vsnl.com • *website:* www.atfullcircle.com

Print & typesetting : SCANSET
J-40, Jorbagh Lane, New Delhi-110003
Tel: 24620063, 55654197 Fax: 24645795

Printed at Dot Security Press Pvt. Ltd., Delhi-110028

PRINTED IN INDIA
01/09/02/03/11/SCANSET/SAP/DSP/DSP

HOMAGE

Homage to the sages of humanity, our teachers, the donors of our philosophy, those travelers in time who were born centuries ago yet come to our day, making us also travel in time by calling us to their age. Homage to the adults of humanity who stand tall and look in compassion at us playing with the toys of our littleness and to the saints of all and no religions, our homage.

Homage to the God-incarnations, the Word become flesh, who come down speaking many languages to many lands in many centuries, whenever virtue is on the decline. They are master-ventriloquists who spoke elsewhere then, but we hear them here and now across the gulfs of time and civilizations. They are the life-force flowing through humanity's collective body, the true homes of our consciousness, the shining suns whose intercession for us is our only light. To them our homage.

Their lives are the only success stories to read, the only archetypes for our dreams. They alone make it worthy for us to belong to the human race, for without them we would destroy like horns of beasts or be torn like horns of dilemmas. From them came to us waves of wisdom, words, confidence in our divine Self; for in them appeared our own divine Self. Them we honour before we meditate. To all gurus of past, present and future, to the saints of all the worlds, our meditation is our homage.

Swami Veda Bharati
Disciple at the Venerable Feet of
Swami Rama of the Himalayas

CONTENTS

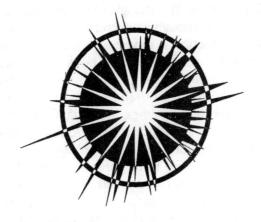

PREFACE

From the words of the poet men take what meanings
please them, but their last meaning points to Thee.
—*Tagore*

"Look at God's poem. It neither decays nor dies," says
the Veda.[1] Men's thoughts touch only the fringes of God's
poem, lacing together this entire universe. The thread of this
lace, Sutrama, runs through all souls. Every now and then a
bead in the rosary recognizes the touch of the thread within
that joins it to other beads. The process of this recognition is
called inspiration. The thought then looks for words and
becomes a composition.

The compositions presented here do not pretend to be

from any specific literary genre. Many idioms are unfamiliar, many words express thoughts not normally ascribed to them in a lexicon. The metre is not always well measured. But the sense of these words is addressed to those who aspire to transcend the senses. The thoughts here are from a personal diary, as it were, thoughts which have poured out unconsciously and sometimes superconsciously. The teachings that comprise the first part of the book are those, by the grace of the guru, that speak to all aspirants wherever they are on the path to the sun. The second part of the book speaks of despairs and longings, to the dark night of the soul and of fulfillment at the touch of light. Although these inspirations and meditations are not chronologically ordered, they were written during three periods. The first group was written from 1954-1965 at the end of which the composition, "I Have Turned My Back To You, Mother," was completed. Nothing was written until 1970 when Mother finally came where I had least expected her to find me. It was then that the second group of compositions was written, among which were the "Songs of Fulfillment." Other meditations included here were written in 1985-86.

A few words about the sun. This body was seven years old when my father first gave me a book of teachings of Swami Rama Tirtha.[2] The most striking stanza in this book was: "Lo, the sun rises in fear of me." A year or two later I read, at my father's instruction, an article in the yoga issue of a well known Hindi magazine, Kalyan. The article was by one of the most outstanding scholars and sages of this century, Shri Gopinath Kaviraj of the holy city of Varanasi, a man who had been initiated into the mysteries of solar science and the tantra. He wrote of the whole universe being a solar field, the energies of which form the various levels of tangible and intangible realities. It seemed then that the solar ancestry claimed by the great kings of India and other eastern countries must refer to the fact that the founders had been initiated into this particular spiritual mystery.

A the age of eleven I memorized the hymns to sun and dawn from the Vedas, the texts which have been handed down orally in the Brahmin families of India for thirty-five or forty centuries. Ten years later, Akhenaton's hymn to Ra (from Egypt of the thirteenth century B.C.) seemed to echo in the same spiritual chamber in which the Vedic rishis were singing of him with golden hand, of him who was traversing the paths between earth and heaven, the single eye of God watching over all things moving and not moving, of him who is the infant of dawn who rises after her sister, night, has given way to light. It is of him that the Brahmins of India recite three times a day:

We take unto ourselves and meditate upon
the beautiful splendour of the sun.
May he inspire our wisdom.

It is the initiation into the meaning of this chant that gives them, with the status of the twice-born, the right and duty to study and pass on the sacred texts.

This golden womb[3] alone is said to be the first and for all times the only teacher of Yoga. Light, too, has been the pre occupation of the mystics and saints for all the centuries since it was revealed to the vision of the poets who sang three hundred and seven hymns to light in the text of the Rig Veda alone. In the Bhagavadgita Lord Krishna shows his universe-encompassing form to the wonder-stricken Arjuna and his form is "brilliant like ten thousand suns risen simultaneously in the sky." No wonder that Krishna said, "I taught this Yoga to the sun (Vivasvat)," the father of Manu who is the archetypal man and personification of all prayers used for meditation.

Many obscure passages in the Yoga texts speak of the solar branch of Yoga. Little do the scholars suspect that the obscurity was intentional, and as a child little did I hope, though I wished much, that a ray of solar light in meditational initiations would ever touch this aspiring but unworthy soul. The rest of the story must be left, again, intentionally obscure though I wish for you a speedy coming to the incarnation when your souls unravel this mystery.

It is my master from the Himalayas only whose thoughts have found words here.[4] All that the reader sees as lofty here comes from the sages and all that is faulty is mine.

ACKNOWLEDGMENTS: A SURYA-NAMASKARA

Because they have performed their solar
salutations daily the Sun, too, has loved them.

This love has reflected in them in the form
of their intangible offerings.

The offerings they have made are their
selfless labors in helping these
Solar Words come to Light.

I, a child and a humble attendant in the
Sun's royal court, express my sincerest thanks
for these labors to: Lalita Arya, Michael Smith,
Derk Amerman.

And any others, please accept my gratitude for
shaping a crystal mirror in which the Sun's rays
may be caught and reflected to many.

Swami Veda Bharati

Editor's Note

The inspirations and meditations in this collection are unique. Swami Veda is not only one of the greatest living spiritual guides in the Himalayan Yoga tradition, but he is a formidable Sanskrit scholar. The combination of these accomplishments made bringing some form of order to this collection a delightful challenge. For, though, on the surface, the inspiring compositions included here are beautiful and edifying, they also arise from a comprehensive knowledge of a plethora of Sanskit texts in the Hindu Tradition attested to in the footnotes, which demonstrate the spiritual and scholarly depth of their origination.

The leading image and concept of the compositions, as the preface indicates, is the sun as it functions in the mysteries of solar science and tantric yoga conjoint with vedanta philosophy. Swami Veda's introductory composition, "Voices of the Sun," tells us that the inspirations in this collection are literally from the sun, streaming like rays from the sun and only given word and form by Swami Veda. All Vedic paths, whether of solar science, tantra, or any other of the many schools and approaches which have sprung up over the centuries, have as their goal the attainment of transcendental consciousness. The method and means for this attainment are the Yogas.

Part I of this book presents, in inspiring prose poetry, timeless teachings, made relevant for us, of the Vedic masters of the sankhya and yoga schools of philosophy, primarily through the five main yogas: karma, bhakti, jnana, kundalini and raja. It is raja yoga, which itself includes aspects of the other yogas, as brought together in the Yoga Sutras of Patanjali, which forms the basis of the teachings in the first section entitled, "Ember Sparks from Sun Rays." These inspiring meditations will also make evident that Swami Veda and the raja yoga tradition embrace all genuine paths to realization be they Christian, Sufi or Buddhist. "Stories and Parables of Power" continue the teachings, while also giving a sense of how much a part of the ancient Sanskrit texts story telling is. Because meditation is the fundamental method in the tradition in general and in raja yoga in particular--often referred to as the yoga of meditation--some of Swami Veda's inspirations that specifically deal with developing the philosophy and practice of meditation have been included under the sections "Mind and Breath" and "Meditation." The section "Marriage of Shakti and Shiva" deals more specifically with the kundalini teachings in tantric and raja yoga. The book is made accessible to the general reader through short footnote explanations where traditional or unfamiliar references are made.

As Swami Veda writes in the preface, the compositions which have been included in Part II reflect many of his own experiences and insights as a traveler along the spiritual path to the light. Thus, they represent a more autobiographical collection than does Part I. They are the teachings lived; lived in longing, despair, questioning, as well as through specific initiatory experiences and fulfillment. The epilogue, "Silence of the Sun" brings us back to the remembrance that this book of inspirations belongs to a transcendent realm of light and quiescence.

Bridging Part I and Part II, at the center of the book, is the composition "Brahman;" Brahman, the supreme unmanifest center of reality from which the manifest is created and called back again in an infinite circular play of light and energy. This beautiful meditation on creation could just as well be called "Divine Mother" for she is also that divine reality from which all of the inspirations in this book emerge to reflect the energy play of the One, the light of ten thousand suns.

Taken from the beginning of Part I through the end of Part II the order of compositions presented offers an archetypically and yet uniquely personal (autobiographical) record of the progressive stages of a swami on the yoga path to realization. The entire book provides an intimate and inspirational teaching guide for those interested in delving into the spiritual path of yoga, in addition to being a collection of unusually beautiful and inspiring writings.

Claudia Crawford

VOICES OF THE SUN

It was a dawn like no other,
Earlier than any ever.
Women, men, children in the village
    of Mihira who were fast
    asleep felt a sudden tremor of consciousness,
And all awoke.
Something flashed in their minds;
Something made their souls smile;
Something made their feet agile.

Some sun rays became the strands of
    a rope around their being,
    and drew them out of doors
    into the streets.

on the mountain peak of the valley
in which they stood,
that beckoned them;
the Light of a Sun never seen before.

Pilgrims, they walked, a silent throng,
    with wonder even in adults' eyes;
    up the twisted and narrow mountain paths,
    they climbed.
Those who had been the most feeble among them
    were the swiftest of foot at this hour.[5]

As they reached the forehead of the mountain[6]
    an orange-robed figure of shimmering lights
    was revealed to their eyes,
    and in that personage they beheld
    the first dawn of the universe
    in which all the suns are born.

Behind His head rose now
    the golden disc of the planet's sun,
    an aura attendant upon the Galactic Saint.

Words were silent,
limbs were still,
eyes fastened to Light.
The very earth seemed like a head
    bowing in homage to the one
    who eternally fulfills her longing.

In this Light now
    there was no east or west,
    no low or high
    and the Light was the same as the peace of the Infinite.

The throng moved close to touch

The throng moved close to touch
    the dust from the Sun's holy feet
    to their forehead,
    but the immaculate feet were not upon the ground,
    nor could they be felt,
    for the fingers only passed through
    a configuration of Light.
    The personage cast no shadows.[7]

Each spirit felt lifted aloft
    as if it were wind,
    yet their wings were weighted
    with one heavy rock, one question:
    "Who? What?
    From where are you?"
No lips moved, but the answer was
    a symphony on the strings of Spirit
    in which the many had become one.

"Know me the Sun Incarnate,
the Golden Womb,
    in which your consciousness is conceived
    and becomes a fetus.
I am He who taught the Father of the first Man.
I am Christ, Kalki[8] and all Messiahs.

At this very moment I make an appearance
    to the inhabitants of all the worlds,
    the worlds as many as ray-hairs on my body.
I come always to dwell among you when you so wish;
    make your hearts my hearths,
    and ask of me whatever you will."

He spoke of many modes of being,
    spoke in their minds.
    Often though, their minds gave vent

yet He loved them for
their imperfections, their sorrows.[9]

Often one knew not which 'I' he spoke of--
His own perfectly joyful
or of their crying, craving egos
and their journeys--as His own.
Said He, "Am I not incarnate in you?
In all your voices it is I who speak!"

Hear then, the gifts
of the intangible wrapped in the tangible;
of Light wrapped in darkness;
of words enwrapping silence.
Hear the Silence of the Sun
that rises from behind the peak of the mind.

PART I

EMBER SPARKS FROM SUN RAYS

LIGHT

The earth is a light. The sky is a light. The beauty of your skin, the softness of your child's cheek, the love in your eyes is a light. The light has become a leaf, a twig, a tree. Light flows as a river from a mountain of light. Whatever you do not experience is not light. All the rest is waves in a sea of light, the light that is the infinite delight, the bliss of God. The lake of Truth and mirage of falsehood is all light.

The song you hear is a light to your ear. The sweet taste is a light to your palate. Love is the light of your heart as meditation is the light of your soul. Light wears many garments, and of these your prayer is the brightest. The sound that is the wave of the universe, the word that is the soul of God, is your inner light wearing the body which is an outer layer of light.

Why would you worship darkness when your eyes are made to see only light? Set aside your dark angers and deep depressions. Hold still for a moment, fellow wave of light; be still. Do you see how the winds of your agitation calm down and the resolute light illumines your mind again? On the altar of the light of True Knowledge, then, burn the light of Love.

From this day may you walk as a being of light. Wherever you tread, leave your footprints of light. Let light alone be your delight. Light.

I AM CALLING YOU

I am calling you. May I speak with you,
you hidden way over there,
you concealed so deep inside?
O, how shall I call You?
If you had a name, I would shout it;
or a size, I would call, "short one, tall one...."
"Young one, old one," would I call if you had an age.

O you, a flicker of light,
waiting in layers of grey dust,
hiding between sheafs of clouds and the clear sky.
I stand outside your cave
inside a cave, inside a cave, inside a cave.[10]
You peek through a crevice from time to time;
the crevice is an eye.
You hear me through the hole of this ear;
you step out for a brief moment
and I lightly brush against the magnet of your fingers.

"Come soul, meet my soul,
and let all magnets of life join in meditation,
and know that this field is but One."
In this day's meditation
may your light find its Cosmic magnet,
may the Union of Heavenly Light
with the Light of your consciousness bring you peace.

WHY SUFFER HUMAN LONELINESS

Why suffer human loneliness,
    when you can enjoy divine solitude?
Why suffer the feelings of confinement,
    when you can rejoice in the meditative cave
    of the heart?
Why look at the shadows under a tree,
    when you can see the light coming through the leaves?
Why make enemies, when you can make friends?
Why hate, when you can love?
Why weep, when you can smile?
Change your obstacles into boons.
Change your tears into smiles
    through love, faith and understanding.
If you meditate on the source of your solitude
    and your loneliness, of your tears and your laughter,
    you will find a stream of divine light flowing
    through you and melting away the frozen darkness
    of life.
Look up to the sun today,
    and take that light and splendour into your soul.

May the corona of your soul touch all the earth.

CUT THE TREE OF CRAVINGS

The hungers you filled this morning returned at noon.[11] The cravings you satisfied at night came back at dawn. There is no end to desires that haunt you. Why seek only the satisfactions that awaken ever new painful hungers? Why not satisfy the first and the last craving, the craving of the soul to find itself?

A year or two ago, you had a problem and you said, "If only this problem could go away, I would be happy." That problem went its way...but, are you happy? Each day you try to cut off one leaf, and a hundred new leaves sprout. Why not uproot the entire tree? The loss of your knowledge of your true Self[12] is the darkness in which grows the poison tree of craving. Do you not see that all your search for things outside of you is in reality a search for the forgotten perfection of your divine Self?

When you come to know the eternal perfection of the divine will, divine knowledge and divine action of your divine Self, then you will cease to crave and suffer. You will cease to wish, and begin to will.

This day I wish you the return of your divine freedom of will.

PACKAGES OF PLEASURE AND PAIN

Are you in pain? Do you seek pleasure? Do you wish a gain, and to avoid all loss? Do you expect victory, without any defeat? Perhaps you do not know that life comes in packages of pleasure and pain.

These packages are presented to you at certain junctions along your journey, and the choice is all yours. Whichever package you choose has a little of the bitter and a little of the sweet. If you wish to conquer a high peak, understand that a deep valley lies in its shadow. If you could go back and exchange your present package for another, your joy and your regret would still be in the same proportion as now.

In your mind you carry the sum total of all your thoughts and acts. These are the seeds from which today's trees of pain and pleasure have grown. From this day, plant the seed of a sweeter fruit in the soil of your mind, and the contents of the package presented to you in your future journeys will change for the better.

May you plant this day a seed of the sweeter fruit.

YOU ARE THE CENTER

"How are you?" is a question which has become synonymous with "How are things?" "Things are going well" has become a statement of one's own well being. Are you things?

Know then, that you are the center and the prime mover of your environment. The well and the ill of your spirit radiate the waves and frequencies of your consciousness and re-order your surroundings. Your ill and your well order their ill and their well, but they are powerless to alter your states, as iron filings sprinkled on a magnet are not capable of changing the pattern of magnetic waves.

Be the flowing water that smooths the furrows and evens the uneven terrain and, through time, reshapes even the hard rock. Be the spiritual hand that changes cotton into cloth. Be also the warp and the woof and the very stretch of that velvet and silk you have made of your life. Provide a perfectly woven cloak of well being for your spiritual Self.

WALK IN LIGHT

When you wake in the morning, take your previous night's failures, dreaded dreams and darkness; stand before the sun, and make them a burnt[13] offering into the sun's flames. Then, walk in light.

When you take a cleansing shower, let all the rivers of this earth and all the streams of solar lights dwell in the flowing waters. Make your mind so that all its impurities and petty malices are washed off and you emerge a newborn, to look at all things afresh. Then, walk in light.

Sitting for your meditations, take a breath of fire and burn your hidden, private, envious, ungenerous evil person, who is made up of wrong thoughts, false words, poisoned foods and undirected deeds. Yes, burn him inside you and with an expelled breath scatter his ashes to the winds. Then rise, and walk in light.

In the evening take your day's concerns and hurts, depressions and pleasures, and the shadows of falsehood; stand before the setting sun, and burn them in the flames. Then find your inner sun, and repose in its light. Even at night rest in light.

THE HUMAN NATION

Stand on a bridge and see the river flow. Not one of the waves that rise and fall remains the next moment, but the river continues. Through all the flux and phases of life the stream of your meditative Self weaves its way as through a changing terrain.

Why do you think that your view and your feeling of this moment alone is the truth and that others are not entitled to the enjoyment of their truths? A true temple of God has shrines to all deities.[14] A man of meditation enriches his mind with a love for the music, liturgy, ritual, religions and cultures of all lands. Are not your eyes a shrine to the sun-god, your tongue an altar to Sophia and Sarasvati?[15]

All the waves that have arisen or shall arise on all the surfaces of the river are included in that river's name. So to close yourself to any culture's beauty or to any religion's ritual is to amputate the mind.

I wish your meditation of this day to lead you to a participation in the beauty of all cultures. May you open your soul to the divine truths that have been revealed to the chosen nation, the human nation.

THE FACES OF TRUTH ARE MANY

When you reject something, do not reject it entirely, for what you reject today you may accept another day. What you dislike do not dislike totally, for another day it may suit your liking. Aversion is another name for attraction. What one layer of you seems absolutely averse to, another layer is attracted to.

The quality named tolerance means that you do not regard the word "truth" to mean your views of this moment, for the faces of truth are many, though you have seen the profile of only one of them. Remember that your "this moment" is only a little of the truth. When you are enjoying the light of the day, do not condemn the night, for in a few hours the peace of the night will give you rest. When you are at peace in the night, remember that in a few hours the sun's hand will touch you to awaken you. The night and the day are two faces of truth.

Someone who stands on the peak sees many trails coming to the top, but one on the forest trail does not see the parallel path. In your temple, in your church, let all cultures flourish. Let each person be guided on his trail by the one at the peak. Let the bee of your mind gather honey from all flowers.

I wish you this day a view of the paths of truth from the Peak.

TRUTH AND LOVE

To reduce Truth to the level of an opinion is darkness. To present a mere opinion as Truth is greater darkness. To call changing emotions love is death, and to see that death as life is even greater death.

Truth and love are inseparable, and they are never changing. To attribute change to them is to live in ignorance. The underlying reality behind all realities is never altered, as the ocean remains the same though many waves arise and subside on the surface.

To separate Truth from love is to separate awareness from feeling. To pursue Truth is to love all.

Do not let your love be a service only to your desire,[16] but let it serve the harmony of Cosmic Truth. Grow together with those you love, and if the aim of your love is to help each other realize union with God,[17] then your love will progress toward the changeless. In so reaching the realm of Permanence, your love will pass all its tests.

PLEASURE AND PEACE

When does pleasure become a vice?

When you depend upon it for all your joy and all your sustenance.

When you are no longer free from attachment as you enjoy pleasure, it becomes your vice.

How can you change your pains into pleasures? When pain is accepted like the rubbing of a sandal on a pilgrim's foot, a stone on the pathway, and like the weariness that comes to all things lesser on the way to reaching all things higher; then your pain becomes your pleasure.

A large bird snatches a wriggling worm from a little bird's mouth; the little bird's helpless lack of freedom is its pain. The same bird pecks another worm, flies to its nest, and a tiny baby mouth snatches the worm; then it is the mother's pleasure. Hold fast to what is destined to be lost and you are in pain; lose it of your own accord and your joy is abundant.

I wish you this day the true knowledge of dependence and freedom and the discernment of pain from pleasure.[18] I wish you that true pleasure and peace.

BE WHAT YOU CAN BE

Be what you can be, and never any less. Do your utmost and you will become what you wish to become. Your highest potential will be reached and your actions will reflect perfection, when you act from what you are.

Being witnesses doing.[19] Be a viewer, even a referee, and not a participant in the battle between your divided ego. Know, thus, the action in inaction, and master inaction through action. This skill will rejoin you with your deepest One.

Glory never attends upon one who has not wearied himself. Be an ascetic on this path. Pick up your burdens and walk, for he who sits sins. He who walks blossoms, and his soul picks the flower. The Sun walks with him, and never tires of ripening the fruit which is the product of his labours.

He who dwells in sleep dwells in the Dark Ages of Iron and Stone. As he yawns to wakefulness, he is yet in the Saturnian Copper Age. When he stands, he enters the Silver Age, lit with a full moon.[20] Then walk toward your perfect being, where the Golden Age of Meditation dawns on you with Solar Light.

I wish you this day a healing and a joining, a reaching of equilibrium through meditation in action.

DECLARE YOURSELF A FOOL

One may easily learn to appear reverent and pious, but for the reverent to become irreverent only for a day calls for greater self-control.

Purity may be white but beauty is colourful. Has not God Herself renounced her transcendental station to become this colourful universe? Just for a day, His day? Learn to throw a sprinkle of colour on the white surfaces of your piety. Rub rose petals on the faces of friends and dance with those who thought you their enemy. Their ridicule of you is an act of God's grace, and the chuckling clown inside you is also the Divine Incarnate.

If you aspire to be wise, first declare yourself a fool,[21] or else your wisdom will evaporate and leave you a fool. Remember, if silence is pure, laughter too is white.[22] It is easy to hold back laughter, but in a serious world it is difficult to generate it.

This day I wish you all the colours of the universe and the galactic guffaws of God's open spaces. Come to me today, any day, with a bundle of your choicest insults, and I will squirt coloured water on you.[23]

19

DIVINE JOY

You are a young man, young woman—handsome, beautiful, attractive. All the treasures of this earth, all the gold mines and diamonds, are your possession. You are the sole ruler of this earth, with all men, all women under your power, responding to your passions. That is the highest ambition that you can have. Call it a single unit of human pleasure.

Withdraw to a meditation where no thoughts intervene, no desires arise. One minute of that meditation is a single unit of divine pleasure, divine joy. Multiply your units of human pleasure by a billion; they are not equal to that one moment of dispassion, that one moment of desirelessness of a meditative wise man.

When you have become wise, all your ambitions and passions, all your present pursuits of human fulfillments, will become as pitiable in your eyes as the tiny grain of sugar in an ant's mouth is to the eyes of a human. The scale of the ant's effort and your effort may be different, but the ratio is the same. Why, then, run after tiny grains of sugar with ant-like feet, grasping and grabbing? Even if you have gathered all things you desire, your desires will not come to an end.

I wish you this day not a billion units of human pleasure, but one single unit of Divine Joy.

WASH THE MIND

Cool the world when I am warm. Warm the world when I am cold. Cover the eyes of all creatures because I am naked in shame--so plead those whose center of being is out in the world and not at the center of the golden triangle of the heart. Warm yourself when you are cold. Bathe yourself when you are hot. Cover your own body to conceal your shame and the world around you will do likewise, so say the sages. The earth is full of thorns and pointed pebbles, but how will you cover its entire surface? When the soles of your own feet are shod with a square foot of leather, you tread a covered earth.[24]

Wash the mind, and the world is clean. Calm the mind, and the world is at peace. Swallow the honeyed pill of the sacred name and let it dissolve into every channel of your being, and all sickness will find its cure. Washing, calming, nourishing and healing your own mind is the most selfless deed you can perform, because the current of mind that flows through you is the same as the consciousness of all.

I wish you this day a purified, calm and nourished mind so that you may find a world full of peace.

"I AM"

When you say: "I am walking, I am seeing, I am hearing," behind those diverse experiences and actions there is a common denominator: "I am." Each action flowing from you to the surrounding persons and objects and each experience from them to you begins with the affirmation: "I am." All those actions and experiences are tangible and can be analysed, but "I am" is the feel of your being, the being of the force field that you are.

Every day, before launching the boat of your body, before rowing it with the oars of your mind across the flowing rivers of actions and experiences, stand on the tranquil banks of your soul for a moment and know that: "I am." Close your eyes. Seal your lips. Still your tongue and say in your mind: "I am." Then ask yourself: "who is that declaring this I-ness, this being? Who whispered from which depths of the well of my existence: 'I am?'" This is truly your only question.

May your meditation give you the answer that answers it all.

ALL IS TRUTH

From your premises this would be the obvious conclusion; this is what it looks like from where you are standing. From where I stand, however, the angle is narrower; it looks different. From my premises the conclusion drawn is just the opposite.

What does Chichen-itza or Borobudur or Tajmahal or Notre Dame look like from a supersonic jet? Does it look the same as from an adjacent park or hill?

Take a solid cone and turn it slowly in your hand; is it a triangle, a circle, or an ellipse?

Ports of call, customs, tariffs, passports, visas--each locus presents a new point of view. Whose country is truth?

None of these is truth—complete truth—and truth cannot be incomplete. Incomplete cannot be truth. There is nothing opposite or contradictory. Day and night: one cycle. Summer and winter: one year. Not only are days and nights distinct, but also the dawns and twilights of merger. I and my enemy, the martyr and the assassin, Gandhi and Godse, Jesus and Judas.[25]

All is complementary. All is truth.[26]

This day may you see truth as a complete circle.

YOUR PROBLEMS WILL BE VERY LITTLE

Every morning is a creation of God,
    the spring of the new year, your childhood.
Every midday is the continuity of that creation,
    the summer of the year, and your youth.
Every evening is the dissolution of the Universe.
It is the winter of your years, the evening of your lifetime.

The grass is akin
    to the tallest shoots of bamboo.
And to crush an ant with your feet,
    is to be crushed by the elephant's foot yourself.

See this order in the Universe and how it affects you,
    your life, your problems.
Your realization will be the dawning of the Great Truth
    that everything is a part of the whole Cosmos.
Then your little problems will be very little;
    then the Truth will be very great.

WHO WATCHES WHILE YOU SLEEP?

At night do you ever say to someone, "Please turn on the lights so that I may see my dreams more clearly"? In what light do you see your dreams? That light is no candle flame. It is your own very Self, for you are a self-luminous being, the source of your body's vitality, the origin of your mind's awareness. This Self never sleeps.

Even though the weary shallow surfaces of the mind succumb to rest, there is someone other, ever-wakeful, ever-watchful. There is someone other who governs your heartbeat and your breath, who prevents you from falling from your bed during your worst nightmares, and who wakes you to the distress cry of your child in the next room. Someone other.

Ask yourself the question "Who am I?" Who utters this word, "I"? Whose light gives you the awareness to say the word, "I"? As you begin to answer this question, you will begin to dive deeper than the shallow surfaces of your mind and go to the true home of consciousness, with its free volition, from where flickers the light of the word "I."

I wish you today identification with the silent watcher within, your true Self.

THE TRUE MIRACLE

Indeed, you have wrought many miracles. You have sent ships into space, machines to Mars, and men to the moon. Iron and all the alloyed metals have made such progress through your touch, for the power of the Infinite dwells within you, flows through your mind, through your hand. Though material things have made much progress through you, what progress have you made yourself?

Do you measure your inner development by the complexity of your machines? Are you more advanced inwardly than the citizens of Egypt, Greece, or ancient Rome?

Can you calm your anger? Can you pull yourself out of a state of depression? Can you prevent ulcers from occurring? If you were alone on an uncolonized planet, could you heal your body or assuage your loneliness? Can you slow down your heartbeat, lower your blood pressure, speed up your digestion, or slow down your breath? Can you observe the processes of your own mind and discover how the voice of intuition may speak through you? Can you mend the splits in your heart?

Until you can do these things, how can you say that you have made progress? Only when you have walked in the light of your inner Self will you have made the true progress that is of supreme importance.

Sit back, ponder a moment, and resolve to make such progress within.

I wish you this day a great leap forward. God bless you with strength.

WALK THROUGH THE DARKNESS

Do you fear the forms of formless worlds? Do you fear ghosts, satans, devils? Only a weak mind is affected by these thoughts. Only a weak mind is open to the influence of these non-beings.

You are a being of light, a being of illumination, dwelling in the clay house of the body with the five doors and windows of the senses. You are a self-luminous flame that casts its light on its surroundings, but on which no shadow can be cast. Not even the shadow of the body can make your light dwindle even by a whit. You can see through your eyes how that light shines.

You, an immortal being, afraid of mortality? You, the spiritual being, afraid of losing the prison house of flesh?

However small a flame, have you ever heard it complain in the face of a room full, or a hall full, or a cave full of darkness, saying "Oh, I am so afraid because the darkness might smother me. I am so small, and the darkness is so vast."

Have you ever walked with white clothing into a room filled with darkness? And has the darkness any power to leave a trace of blackness on your immaculate whiteness?

You are a being of light— ever pure, ever-wise, ever-free. Walk through the darkness and shine forth.

I wish you this day the recognition of your inner light.

SONG OF SELF

Cut a piece of empty sky[27] a few yards square with a pair of scissors. Roll it up like a bolt of cloth and use it for a wrap to cover your body. Make a bow with the horns of a rabbit. Adorn it with flowers of the sky and give it to the natural son of a barren woman.[28] The day you can accomplish these impossibles, that very day, you can hope to find peace anywhere, knowing your own Self.

You cannot hope for freedom without the knowledge of your true Self. Look at your outer self. Place your hand on your heart and say, "Whatever is here is elsewhere. What is not here is nowhere else."[29] If a speck of dust looks like a star to you, there must first have been a star within you. There can be no recognition of what is without unless it is within.

Know, then, that knowledge, from the smallest speck of dust to a star, comes first from the knowledge of your true Self.

May you this day find knowledge of that Divine Self who dwells both in the speck of dust and in the star.

GREATER THAN THE UNIVERSE IS THE SELF

Greater than the universe, and more minute than an atom's nucleus, is your Self.[30] If the light of all the suns from all the galaxies were condensed into a diamond head, that diamond head is your Self. Unchanged in the changing personality, without pain amidst suffering, untouched by temptations of false pleasure, is your Self.

The sun in your eyes, the symphony in your ears, the roses in your nostrils, the winds on your skin, are of the Self. The Self that is the life-force has given words to the tongue, drumbeat to the heart and fire to your stomach.

Let your awareness go deeper than the form, sound, touch and taste and you will know that you are not the eyes, ears, skin and the mouth. Nor are you the impressions received through them. Free of all oscillations, without form, a flowing current of living consciousness, is your true Self. That true Self is God. To know that Self is to worship God.

This day I wish you an acquaintance with that God which is your own deeper Self.

STORIES AND PARABLES OF POWER

Do you seek power? Do you wish to conquer your world? Is the whole world your opponent, your adversary? Do you seek the power of wealth and control over others? Does the world seem full of unsympathetic, unjust people, always criticizing you, attacking you? Are your anxieties and worries of the past or of the future?

Once upon a time an ancient king had a hall of mirrors built in his palace to entertain his guests. One morning after a long night of celebration, after the banquet was over and all the guests had left, the king's pet dog wandered into this hall of mirrors. He saw himself surrounded by a thousand other dogs, baring their fangs, snarling, barking. With each of his barks was the echo of a thousand others. The valiant dog defended himself all alone from those thousand opponents. In the morning the king's dog was found laying on the floor, totally exhausted and near death.

What would have been the best way for the king's dog to make those thousand other dogs cease barking at him, to make those thousand other dogs cease attacking him? Only to sit back and stop baring his own fangs, stop barking, stop attacking. For with each attack he made, a thousand of his own reflections lunged back at him, robbing him of life.

To find peace and true power in your life, sit back a moment and be still. Be quiet, be tranquil, and the world will cease to attack you.

Once a great woman saint was passing through a forest infested with robbers. With her was a noble woman bedecked with gold and jewels. When the robbers attacked, the saint took the jewelry of her companion, gave it to the leader of the robbers and said, "Here my son." When she said "my son," there was such a depth of love in her voice that the bandit chieftain wept. "From the time I was a child, no one has called me thus, son - and so lovingly. My mother died when I was so young " From that time on the leader of the robbers became her true son and followed her everywhere. Later he himself became a great saint. Such was the power she had over him.

There is a power which is not the power of wealth and riches nor ego. Neither is it a power exercised to control others. There is a power that is in loving eyes, the power to convert an enemy into a friend. There is a power in a gentle touch of the hand, soothing injuries, bringing light to eyes that were blind, healing the unhappy, making the lonely rejoice.

Once upon a time an emperor posed this question to his advisors: "Here, I have drawn a line on this board. Without touching this line in any way, please make it shorter." After all his counselors had pondered over the problem and had given up, his wisest minister approached the writing tablet. He drew a line parallel to the emperor's, but just a little longer, and said, "Your Majesty, your line is now shorter."

If you always seek to shorten the lines drawn by others, you will not win your battles. Draw your line from your own genius. Tap your own resources. Apply your concentration with an inner relaxed mind. Center your mind. Your creative energy is waiting to burst forth. There is within you an eternal genius waiting to express itself. Sit back and listen to him. Draw your line with full concentration, without comparing it to the lines of your competitors. Then you will have drawn the longest line of all.

When the famous Macedonian conqueror, Alexander the Great died in Babylonia, he said to his retinue, "When you bury me, cover me with a shroud. But place both my hands out of the shroud with the palms up and put a pinch of ashes in each, so that the world may see and know what the conqueror of the world is able to take with him."

If you seek conquest, seek first the power of self-conquest. Then seek that power which is service to others. Seek the power to benefit and comfort the many, for only such a power will be remembered. And even if you yourself do not gain from this power, many years hence generations of people will continue to benefit from it, and you will be blessed.

Once upon a time there were three young men, two of whom were not yet born and one who was not yet conceived. Suffering from the pain of miserable poverty, they decided to migrate from the city named Empty. On the way, feeling weary, they rested under the shade of three trees, two of which had never been planted and the third which has not yet grown. Having rested there and eaten of the fruits thereof, they came to three rivers, two of which had no water and the third which had run dry. They quenched their thirsts from these rivers and then crossed over in three boats, two of which had never been built and the other which had no bottom. After a long arduous journey, the three youths came to a city called Future and settled down in three houses, two of which had never been built and the third which had no walls. They lived in Future city ever after.

Your present anxieties and worries are as baseless as the unreal cities in the parable. Although your anxieties and fears and sorrows are here presently, the bad events which you base them on are forever gone or have not yet arrived. Clear your mind and in the light of your clear mind you will see that in this very moment there are solutions to the problems which have already gone or not yet arisen.

Which power do you truly wish? That which involves you with the false reflections of the snarling dogs of the world? Or the power of peaceful tranquillity which draws people to you? Which love do you really wish for? The phantom love of wealth and riches or ego and its control of others? Or the infinite power of the heart? Do you wish to suc-

ceed by competing against the lines drawn by others? Or do you wish to blaze forth in the creative expression of your own eternal genius? Do you wish to conquer the world and gain only ashes? Or the enduring powers of self-conquest and of one who has served? Do you wish to create and live in fear of the ghosts of past and future? Or to dwell in the city of divine clarity of the moment?

I wish for you the true powers of tranquillity, love, inner genius, service and divine clarity of each moment.

GO STILL

Amidst all your cries and laughter let your mind take a moment off, and go still. Look at this moment, this moment alone, and go still.

This would not mean to silence all your thoughts, emotions and words. Just trace them to the silence which precedes all speech, and go still. There is a minutely brief moment of quiet from which a wave rises and into which it merges. As you observe a wave, observe also its quiet source and the silent end, and go still.

Each breath that you take begins and ends with a moment's pause. Fill that gap when you breathe, fill it with the silence of meditation, and go still.

Before you burst with anger, before you let go of your passion, hold your mind, fix it on a quiet within you. Then even in the midst of your anger and passion you will find a stillness that will make your emotion into a well wielded tool, a tool to help you be still.[31]

At this moment, dive within you, dive to depths, and go still.

A MAGNET

Some people are afraid to slow down. They want to remain perpetually active, for activity means to them winning, success, conquest. But let me ask you: "Do you understand activity and passivity?" Take a magnet. Let it sit. Around it sprinkle some iron pins and needles. The pins and needles, it is seen, rush towards the magnet while the magnet apparently sits still doing nothing. But which of these two, the magnet or the pins, is actually active?

If you think that activity means much movement, then you also probably think that energy means great restlessness. Like the magnet, the deep part of your being contains restful energy. It looks passive outwardly, but inwardly it is dynamic.

When you cultivate such inward energy, you no longer need to be perpetually active. You sit like a magnet and draw to yourself the situations, circumstances, environments and relationships that you require. These things come helplessly rushing to you like those pins and needles towards the magnet.

I wish you the magnetism of inner dynamism--the energy that is creative and yet restful. God bless you with such magnetism.

WATERS OF TRANQUILLITY

Sometimes be quiet. There are two kinds of pleasures in the world: the pleasures of excitation and the pleasures of tranquillity.

In the pleasures of excitation there is much outburst of energy, much rising, a feeling of power; and then there is a great letdown.

In the pleasures of tranquillity there is a quiet dynamism like that of a magnet. It is an inward satisfaction. It is even, not jarring, jerking, jagged. It is smooth, gentle, ever-flowing, like clear water in which you can see all that is hidden within you.

Sit by the still waters and be quiet. When you come out of your contemplation, you may not have found answers to your questions, but many questions afterwards will have been resolved. When there is a vengeful desire in you to get even, get even-minded. And like water, that always returns to its own even level, your life will flow even and smooth.

I wish you such smoothness of character. God bless you.

SILENCE

The silence of speech is not silence.
Silence of mind is true silence.
Silence is the infinity of the Word that is God.
In the beginning was that silence; that silence was in God.

When words are spoken from a mind that is truly still,
    silent and tranquil, they are inspired words, sending
    their power echoing for centuries around the globe.
In the silence of your meditation such words shall arise.

In the practice of silence, only truth is spoken.
Speak truth; speak that which is pleasant.
Do not speak unpleasant truth; do not speak pleasant
    untruth.[32]
This is the ancient law of silence, that all spoken words
    come true[33] when they arise from the depths of silence.

LIGHT AND LOVE

God is light and love.

The love that your heart longs for is the recognition of your Self in all Selves, and the recognition of all Selves in your Self. This light and this love is so sublime that there are no words to express it. Only the deepest state of meditation can show you the depth of that universe of love which is in you.

Love without questioning. Love without analysing. Love unconditionally. When you love ask, "What can I give?" Do not ask, "What can I receive?" Do not call your craving for reassurance or your selfish needs by the name of love. Let love flow unhindered from soul to soul. Give of yourself without expectations. Give up a little of your freedom to the other, and allow your love to bind you fast together. The spirit of your love should be the same as Christ's love for Mary Magdalene.

Let your love for every person be a worship of God.
There is only light. There is only love.

I wish you this day a shower of such love and an expanded awareness which embraces all others in a circle of divine light and love.

GENTLENESS OF HEART

Why smoulder and smoke when you can burn bright even for a brief moment?[34] Do not play long in the shallows. Dive deep even for the duration of only a heartbeat. Do not meditate for long if you cannot, just go to utter stillness, even for the space of a single breath.

If someone excites you, hold yourself still. Something entices you? Pause just a moment before you rush headlong. Do a kind deed to someone who constantly irritates you. Declare yourself in the wrong when you know you are in the right, and face an angry opponent with a disarming smile.

Even through your most hostile acts, let a basic friendliness show. Even in the middle of a violent quarrel, do some little gentle deed to signal that in a larger perspective all is love somewhere. Deal with life firmly but gently as you would hold a baby.

And if you can follow all this advice you will become so attractive to the world that birds will alight on your shoulders, wolves will cease to bite, and opposing armies will lay down their swords in your presence.[35]

I wish you this day the gentleness of heart which is true love and peace. May your subconscious, receiving the love of the superconscious, invite the love of all.

BOW BEFORE ALL LIVING BEINGS

Bow before every man, for you do not know in what guise God will make an appearance.[36] Clasp you hands like two flower petals, bring them near your heart, bend your head and say, "All the love of my heart, all my head's intuition and intelligence, all my power of action, I offer you like a flower on the altar. I worship the God within you."[37]

If you cannot see God in a stone,[38] you will not see Her in the sun. If you do not see Her in the sun you can see Her neither in the Self nor in Christ. Know, then, that the heaven in a rock that lies at the bottom of a stream[39] is the same as the angels who sing every moment in your breath.

So you may know that leonine nature can be tamed, cats were given to you. Babies are granted so you may see the innocence and unblemished purity of your own soul. As horses are broken and bridled, so senses can be ruled. And a cow gives you milk all your life to remind you that the maternal love you received as a child flows unceasing from the breast of all beings.[40]

Share, then, this earth with the Deity that is in the cat and the lion, the horse and the cow, the baby whale and the ant's egg. Remember that a dog, too, smells incense herbs in the grass and a tiger's eyes are candles burning on God's altar. Bow before all living beings, for in their guise God makes Her appearance.[41]

SELF-CONQUEST

You wish to win your battles.
If you really want to win, your first victory must be over
  yourself.
The conquest of oneself is the only true conquest.

Can you calm down when you are agitated?
Can you slow your breath when you are excited and are
  breathing fast?
Can you silence your chattering mind for a moment
  so that you can listen to
  the intuitive messages
  that are waiting to break through the curtain
  of mental noise?

If you can answer, "Yes" to these questions, you have
  already won your battles.

I wish you this day, with the conquest of yourself,
  a meditation on your innermost resources.

GIVE WITH A THOUSAND HANDS

Do you want to conquer? Do you want to win? Everything has a price. For every pleasure you must undergo some pain. What price are you willing to pay for your conquests? Do you want a success that will leave you ulcerated, that breaks your family apart, that leaves you all alone, that busies you so that you cannot sleep at night? What kind of success is that?

True success is when you not only have what you require in the world, but also health in your body, relaxation in the nerves, happiness in the heart, gentleness in your voice, peacefulness of mind, joyousness in the family and the understanding of great truths.

So, when you seek outer success, do not lose sight of these inner successes. Do not barter them as a price for mere material comforts. Do not be a success in the world and a failure within your person.

Yes, go gather your material goods with a hundred hands if you so chose, but give with a thousand!

Today I wish you such a complete success in which you prosper and also give richly of the fountain of your most precious internal goods.

WHEN YOU WANT TO GIVE, GIVE

Give way to your human urges. Though you have been conditioned to hide them, do not repress them. When the urge arises in you to give, give. When you have an urge to share, share. If you would like to believe, then believe. If there is an urge in you to seek and honor an elder, then seek and honor an elder. When you desire to worship, why hold back? Worship with your whole heart. When you would like to sacrifice, then sacrifice with a smile.

Give way to your urge to cherish others. Give way to your urge to make others happy. Yes, when you want to be loved, be loved. And when you have the urge to communicate, then drop your fears and communicate. Unite. Search for the intangibles, for that too is a hidden urge within you. And that urge to give softness and gentleness; give them. If you wish to be seen as beautiful, then be seen as beautiful. Be beautiful. When you would rather be smaller, be smaller. What is this pressure to always be great.

Let there be this pleasure in your life that says, "Ah, I caused pleasure. I brought a smile." If you see two person's fighting, catch the eyes of one and smile. You will have diffused the tension. Amidst frustration, seek accord. Sow accord. Yes, give pleasure.

Yes, give way to your urges. Do not repress them by that negative which you have often been conditioned to respond to. When you wish to love, love. When you wish to sow accord amidst discord, smile. When you have the urge to give, give.

I wish you the freedom to indulge your divine human urges.

WHAT IS HERE TO ENJOY?

In any situation, do not say to yourself: "Let me see what is here to suffer," but rather: "Let me see what is here to enjoy." The pleasures of mind you will thus receive will more than compensate for the discomfort you may encounter.

If you love the vast ocean and are at present standing only by a lake and miss and suffer the absence of the sea, then you neither have the enjoyment of the sea nor the pleasure of the lake. Enjoy this moment's enrichment while progressing toward the oceans of your future.

If you are not progressing towards the oceans of your ambitions, if you are not seeing the way over your impediments, remember that there is perhaps a wall blocking your intuition from streaming forth into your conscious mind. When the mind is filled with the cobwebs of discontent with the present and worries about the future, you cannot see your way out of the fog. Let the mind relax. Savor the riches of this moment, and in a while answers will come streaming forth.

I wish you this day a meditation that will relax your mind from present discontent and future worry.

THE TREASURE OF YOUR MOMENTS

You have a treasure. Your earthly treasures are counted in units of money but the units of your treasures of life are the moments. The money spent can be earned again but not so the moments spent. Use wisely the moments you have, just as you economise with your monetary resources. Your breaths are your nickels and dimes. If each breath were equal to a nickel, how many nickels have you spent since this morning and how many have you invested in higher awareness?

You want to be a perfect person, a great man, dependent on yourself alone? One not swayed easily by little gusts of wind, not thrown about like a leaf tumbling down, not like dust being plowed under? You want to be a person who chooses his own destiny, his own acts, his own thoughts first? Only if you can choose your own thoughts can you choose your actions and your own future. You will never again wish for anything. You will will your thoughts and actions with your power to will. Your will power. But that comes only by using the resources of your moments wisely. Will your meditative thought to flow on the current of breath and discover that this, your spare moment, is a treasure. Every moment, be, be aware, be aware of your breath of life.

May you prosper; may you be rich in time to meditate.

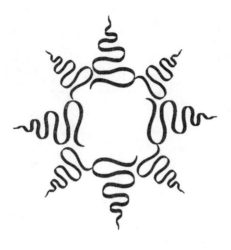

MIND AND BREATH

THE UNIVERSAL MIND

Prophesies, proverbs, and psalms were precious stones mined by the prophets of the past. The golden ideas of eternal wisdom will enrich you also if you have charted well the mine that is your mind. Whether you find coal or diamonds depends on whether you know how to find the right vein and where to dig the shafts.

The history of humankind is the history of human mind. All tools and all toys, all pains and all joys are creations moulded from the matter that is the mind. Man and woman, you are mind. The animal in you is the lesser mind and the God in you the higher mind. The higher mind is consciousness of the sun, in the light of each heart. It is all of the mind—the growth in a blade of grass, the pollination of flowers, the joining of passions and the initiation of spiritual seekers. The mind of God has become this world.[42] World-mindedness is your ego. The surrender of your ego to the higher Self in meditation is the subsiding of a wave into the ocean.

May your mind be tuned to the songs of the Universal Mind. May you become a harmonious note in this cosmic music.

MIND-READING

Many among us would like to become mind-readers. Why would someone want to invade the privacy of others when he would not like his own privacy so invaded? There are many people who are palm-readers and fortune tellers, and many more who seek them out. "What is in my stars?" they ask.

Do the stars control your life? Do the stars direct your actions or is it your own will, the volition of your deepest self-luminous Self?

If the stars control your movement, who controls the movement of the stars? Why not go directly to this same one? And if you cannot reach that same one who guides the destiny of the stars, why not return your gaze to yourself, and there seek the one who creates your destiny?

If you want to become a mind-reader, then begin with your own mind. Can you read your own mind? What are the thoughts you have had since you woke up this morning? Why do you always run out of the castle of your personality, out of the palace of your own mind, stretching begging hands to others? If you return your gaze to your own mind, deep within your recesses, you will come to a core, a pin-point where you are linked to a great Self: your own expanded consciousness whose volition at this very moment may change. your life forever. Pull yourself out of your present dependencies and walk forth with assurance from yourself, with Self-assurance.

I wish your mind freedom, freedom and independence.

THE LINK BETWEEN YOU AND GOD

It is dark underneath the lamp though it illuminates the whole chamber. Your eyes see all things but your eyes you cannot see. You observe changes in your environment but you are not aware of the constant flux that is your personality.

From moment to moment a series of uncounted acts and experiences leaves its imprint on your mind. The sum total of these gives to your mind its dispositions and to your personality a momentum that draws to you your situations like needles to a magnet.

Choose today the person you want to be and you will be choosing the situations you will attract. Learn, for this first, to observe your thoughts. Learn, second, to create your thoughts. Learn, third, to create your environment from these thoughts. Learn, fourth, to remain free of your surroundings by finding the calm eye in the center of your mental storms.

The mind is the barrier between you and your Self, and mind is the link between you and your God.

This day I wish that your barriers of the lost and gone moments of mind become your links with Infinity.

You have dug many mines, mind, and melted many minerals in the crucible of your subconscious. You have criss-crossed many oceans from shore to shore, trading in actions and experiences. You have begged at many kings' courts for favours and gathered much treasure and much trash. What you have thought of as treasure, though, was not always so. In all the things you have pursued and possessed in the past, do you find anything worth more than the price of a broken seashell?[43]

When you sit alone, do you think all your pursuits have been worth their value in time? Why not look now for something truly precious? Why not seek the golden treasure of cosmic beams of light crystallized and gathered in the jar of your unborn and undying person? With all sun rises and sun sets the moments of your life are little by little dissipated; your life span diminishes. Every day, like the Buddha, you too see the cycle of birth, sickness, old age and death moving unceasingly, and yet the wine of delusion you have drunk does not let you wake to your own Self. How many of the interests of your past days do you maintain even this day?

Why not look for a quest that has been with you from the beginning of eternity and will remain with you to the limits of infinity? Enter through the gate of concentration and you will find in the many chambers of your inner palace absorbing interests from which you will never again turn away.

I wish you this day, mind, the discovery of your innermost treasures.

MY MIND, MY CHILD

Mind, why do you act so like a child? Why do you grab at every toy and gleaming tinsel? Why do you wish to horde all these pebbles and lumps in your pouch and then also burden me with their care? How many of my strings of moonlight pearls, my quiet moments, you have unstrung. How many of my laces of sunlight, my illuminated thoughts, you have unraveled, mind.

Mind, why do you not grow to maturity? You know well that you are of human descent with a saintly destiny and yet you join these beasts of malice and petty violence in their pranks against me. You take all the colours and splash them on yourself, one colour now and another the next moment. What a baby's drawing you have made of yourself and you call that experience, mind.

Mind, choose your colours with care and draw your lines. Here the prayer, there the breath, here the light between your eyebrows, there the celestial sound in the right ear.[44] Mind, come let us sit together today--just me, brother breath and you, and let me give you both a beam of my luminosity. My mind, my child, let me make you beautiful.

WATCH OVER YOUR MIND

You mind is your true personality. It shows through all your movements, gestures and words. Your reactions and decisions come from the mind. Every morning you wash your face before you present it to the world. Why not also wash your mind?

The mind is your servant and seeks to favour you who are its master. Watch over the mind and it will cleanse itself; leave it free and it will soil you. Watching the mind constantly is the art of mediation in action. Follow, therefore, four rules of thought and resolve daily:

Wrong thoughts that have arisen I shall eliminate.
Wrong thoughts that have not yet arisen I shall prevent
    from arising.
The right thoughts that have not yet arisen I shall make
    to arise.
The right thoughts that have arisen I shall maintain,
    nourish and help to grow.[45]

With this observance of thought you will become lovable if no one loved you before. You will become attractive if no one was attracted to you before. You will become a magnet if you were mere iron before.

I wish you this day a mind you can watch over, a mind you have cleansed, a mind you magnetise with your spiritual energy and I wish all beautiful thought to your mind.

YOUR BREATH

Your breath is a river that flows between the twin banks of your nostrils. The physical tributary of this river starts in the fire-pool of your solar plexus. The vital spiritual tributary begins in the cave behind your forehead. Through all your expirations and inspirations your vital energy declares: "I am life. I am awareness. I am a being. I am not of depressions and death. I am the very Self of eternal hope."[46]

This, your breath, is a mere waft of breeze if it begins only in the navel and the lungs. When you know, however, its source is in your mind and in turn it generates mental power, it is a ray of sun, a winged soul in flight. Then it says: "I am. I am who I am. Before Abraham was, I am."[47] It sings the hymn of all here and now as a song of eternity.

This day I wish you, through your breath, the knowledge of the changeless in the changing, and of the eternity in this time. I wish you that stillness which comes when you hear for a long time the flow of the mental tributary of breath. May the doors between your eyebrows open to the mental chambers of hidden wisdom and inspiration.[48]

TRANSITIONS

Between two sounds there is silence, between two breaths there is a breathless moment.[49] Between two thoughts there is a mental quiet. That silence, the breathless moment, the mental quiet, is a gate between two walls. You may open it only to friendly thoughts or you may let in a crowd of disheveled rowdies. Your own will is your gate-keeper.

Between two places, two moments, two acts, there is a transition. It is the Christmas between your years. It is the greeting between meeting and parting. You may enter a house with a smirk or a smile. Whether you sow good will or ill will you receive the fruit of your choice.

Then watch your transitions from moment to moment. The length of your thought is the length of your breath. Whatever thoughts and feelings are permitted to enter into your mind through the gates between breaths will sweeten or poison your inner reservoir. Watch your breath, then, and let not the tranquillity and silence of your inner chamber be disturbed by the unwelcome gushes of poisoned thought.

As you wish others sweet dreams in the hours of sleep at night, I wish you sweet thoughts throughout the wakeful hours of your day. Have very bright, full of light, very gentle thoughts for the day, through the day's meditation.

Peace to you.

May that, my mind, be filled with beautiful
and godly thoughts
That which leads humans like a good charioteer his horses,
With reins held far
That heart drawn
May that, my mind,
and godly th

MAY THAT, MY MIND,
BE FILLED WITH BEAUTIFUL AND GODLY THOUGHTS

That which travels far while one is awake,
That which also goes far while one is asleep,
That far reaching one, light of all lights,
May that, my mind, be filled with beautiful
    and godly thoughts.

That with which all the wise men perform their actions,
And the sacrificers perform their priestly duties
    and worship,
That which is the unique, mysterious personality hidden
    within all beings,
May that, my mind, be filled with beautiful
    and godly thoughts.

That which is the absolute knowledge, that which is the
    reservoir of the mind-stuff,
That which is the light hidden in all beings,
That without which no action is performed,
May that, my mind, be filled with beautiful
    and godly thoughts.

That Immortal One, by which all the past, present and
    future of this world is held,
That by which, through which, the sacrifice of the seven
    priests is extended and performed,[50]
May that, my mind, be filled with beautiful
    and godly thoughts.

That in which Knowledge, Action and Music, the three
    branches of wisdom,
Are held as spokes in the hub of a wheel,
That which is the charioteer of my heart,

May that, my mind, be filled with beautiful
    and godly thoughts.

That which leads humans like a good charioteer his horses,
With reins held fast, guided with supreme skill,
That heart dwelling most agile, speediest force of all,
May that, my mind, be filled with beauty
    and godly thoughts.[51]

MIND AND MEDITATION

An unguided mind is a chariot drawn by untrained horses,[52] ready to throw you by the wayside. Only a mind well restrained will keep to your charted path. A mind without meditation is like a diffuse, scattered light illuminating only a corner. But meditative consciousness is a sharp beam cutting through a thick granite-black darkness.

Your dreams, fantasies, visions and wishes are the clutter from a subconscious corner in which spiders of sense impressions have woven their cobwebs. A meditative mind is like an unclouded sky,[53] full of sunlight, like a candle flame, steady, where there is no breeze. Only such a sky is fit for wings. Only such a flame truly gives light. Only such a mind becomes an instrument of freedom.

Make your choice, then, between confusion and clarity, between clouds and sun, between the pleasant and the good. Say to yourself this day: "I have made my choice, in this life, enlightenment. In this very life, a Christlike stature. The Buddhahood, within my allotted number of breaths."

Brother mind, meditate and help me.

Rain-washed fruit,
  stream-washed pebble,
    sun-washed earthling,
      japa-washed mind.[54]
Leaf-sheltered berry,
  tree-sheltered shade,
    moon-sheltered wild,
      guru-sheltered mind.
Om-centered speech,
  Mantra-centered thought,
    point-centered circle,
      soul-centered mind.
Wind-loved mountain,
  breeze-loved hill,
    psalm-loved prophet,
      God-loved mind.
Peel and cast off body-rind,
  all the prana-twists unwind,
  loosen breath-warp power-knots,
  think the gentle no-thought thoughts.
See by heart's eye un-name-numbered,
  un-space-measured, sun-throb-timed,
  saintly, centered, unbound mind.
Sword-edged knowledge, ray-sharp wisdom,
  two wheels treading pathless paths,
    leaving mere mind behind:
      japa-washed mind,
      guru-sheltered mind,
      soul-centered mind,
      God-loved mind.
Trained and tamed, abandoned mind
  on the royal road to God,
    by the souls of stainless kind,
      by the saints of mindless mind.

MEDITATION

MEDITATION MIRROR

My mind, mirror that you are,[55] you are so befogged I cannot see my face clearly. You open all the windows of senses and run about from one to the other, looking out, bringing in all manner of sight and sounds. You distort their truths to me. Why, mind?

Mind, I gave you this agility as I gave vitality to these breaths, and gleams of perception to the senses, and you lead us round and round from cycle to cycle of ignorance and pain, death and rebirth. Can we not become friends, we who share this house of clay, this body, mind?

Mind, shut those windows and sit still, just a while. Do not agitate these breaths. Let them calm down too. Let me cleanse your face and illuminate your eye of wisdom so I may see my own real face clearly, so together we may step off this whirling wheel into a world of eternal stillness. You have been giving care to all else, out there. Just for a moment now, turn around inward and do listen to me. Can we not be friends, mind? Calm down and be still, brother mind.[56]

THE CALL OF YOUR INNER SELF

For whom are you lonely but for your inner Self? Whose calls do you hear but of your inner Self? Your conscience, your guilt, your love are garments your inner Self wears. If you mistake the masks of personality for your inner Self, you will always be lonely, guilty, in ignorance. But if you can throw away the masks you will find your are the face, the mirror and the image also. You are the one who calls and the voice you hear. The one who responds to that voice is also you.

If for some time no inner call comes to you, why do you struggle for it? When the voice calls you, also why do you struggle against it? Give up for a day all things you have gathered, all your impressions, memories, experiences. Stand innocent and untouched before the light which is you on the altar that is you. Then that light will call the Light, that flame will mingle with the Flame.

A man of experiences cannot meditate. Only the innocent meditate.

This day I wish you the loss of all experiences. I wish you the purity of innocence, which is your true peace and Light.

KRISHNA

Your body is a tree upside down.[57] Its roots stretch above, in the head that is the long-haired divine form of the sky, and your branches hang below. Hidden somewhere in the thick foliage sits your Krishna,[58] the handsome one who attracts and charms each and all. He plays his flute, calling in strange notes, and all your cows, the senses, leave their pastures and gather around.

That is your first mediation.

This mischievous Krishna plays yet more strange notes and the dancers and danseuses, your energy currents, come running in all their beauty and gaze at him inside you.

That is your second meditation.

Beyond that is pure bliss. Where can I find a phrase book of the language of that world from which the charming one hails and to which he kidnaps us all while we meditate?

I pray that you are kidnapped by Krishna this day and I wish you a happy voyage to the world of that flute player who will charm you and love you.

DRAW YOURSELF TO YOURSELF

Draw yourself to yourself. Empty your mind of all things from sources outside you and look into your mind for a force that may be entirely yours. A body in meditation is totally relaxed. All muscles are limp, there is no twitching, no movement. The mind has no memories and, therefore, no anxieties. When the mind has no anxieties the breath flows evenly and smoothly. All the hollows of the mind are filled and there are no sharp edges. The brain becomes clear. The thoughts do not arise at random.

That evenness of the mind brings an evenness of emotions, and a quality of equilibrium develops in your personality. That equilibrium may last for a moment or two while in meditation, and initially that is so. But as your meditations prosper they begin to permeate your personality and through all your thoughts, words and physical deeds your natural equilibrium begins to show.

Drain all waters from the Pacific Ocean and fill them with liquid light[59]—these are the unfathomable depths of your mind.

I wish you a dive into the depths of an ocean called consciousness, filled with light.

HEAR THE SONG OF YOUR BREATH

Hear the song of your breath, for it sings of hope, light and life for all your days and nights. In your mind, hear it sing so, as you inhale. Hear it say ham, as you exhale.[60] Through all your inspirations and expirations hear your breath sing soham: "I am He. I am who I am. Before Abraham was, I am." Soham: "I am the eternal life, the winged soul, the solar swan of purity and freedom."

Did you say you were lost? Then let your breath answer soham: "I am the one whom the God of my heart has found." Did you say you were despairing? Then remember your breath singing of life. In your laughter and tears, through problems and solutions, you have a companion— your vital breath.

Hold your mind to your breathing. Feel its streams flowing in your nostrils, its ocean-like tides on the beaches of your brows. Hear it sing soham: "I am." Yes, again, center your mind on the feel of your breath and let its inward currents take you to those depths of your life-force from where your mind arises and into which it subsides.

May your breath take you to that origin of life-currents where silence folds the words away and unfolds sheets of light.

THE MANTRA GLIDES

The mantra glides,[61] soaring through the skies of the breezes of breath in the rarefied atmosphere. In the stratosphere beyond the mind it streaks across the shining cosmic rays, like a falling star descending to our earthly mind. The bells ringing in your ears are not of the bronze of this earth.[62]

A pillar of light rises from the firm ground of your posture and penetrates into heaven. The faith here moves no mountains; it makes steady the fragments of your limbs.

While in subterranean caves, fires burn unseen, volcanoes explode, the underground lakes and streams churn unhindered, the body sits rock-like and the spirit moves. The breath of God gently stirs the reservoirs within.

The waves that strike your shores, the tides that swell from head to toe, the Pacific depths that rise in the voice of Sophia, who makes your mouth her dwelling, sings:

These are your friends from the lands of Eternity.
The journey is not too long, only a few incarnations.[63]
The ocean is not too wide, only a few aeons.

Patience, brother soul, you will reach as others have in the past. When pranas become your friends and your mantra glides in the stratosphere beyond, the mind knows that the other shore is very near and that the boat of your body will reach the land of lands. The land of reality and light.

PROBLEMS OF GREAT MAGNITUDE

If you suffer from many little problems, look for a problem of larger magnitude, and the many little problems will vanish from your view. Answers to little questions are always to be found in large questions. If many minor thoughts battle in your mind, immerse them into an all-absorbing thought.

But where shall I find these problems of great magnitude, these large questions, all-absorbing thoughts? Just breathe gently onto the surface of your mind's reservoir and your mediation will create the currents that will float you to the islands where these magnificent fruits grow. Just blow gently on the surface of your mind.[64]

Do I have the strength to carry such large burdens? To this I say, your little bundles are a lot heavier to carry than the large burdens that the adults of humanity--Christ, Krishna and Buddha--have carried. In your meditation today those saints are silent, and that silence is the voice that will guide you and give you strength.

I wish you that silently meditative strength.

RAYS OF THE SUPERCONSCIOUS

A strange imperceptible poison in you changes the conscious into subconscious. It distorts your images, pollutes the streams of inspiration, holds court with shadows. Whenever an experience enters through the windows of your senses, the subconscious lurking behind the doors alters your perceptions and you find that the residue of your experience is deposited at the bottom of your mind's lake. It misinterprets lights as shadows and misguides your intuition.

The Superconscious alone can cleanse you and make your waters serene and still. When you meditate let the residue of past actions and experiences lie undisturbed. Let the Superconscious cut through your ego like a razor's edge. Let it flash like lightning[65] on the forest trail you are walking. Do not let the hoot of the subconscious disturb you. Let not its fears come to the surface.

I wish for you this day a total loss of your subconscious and of every murky thing that arises from its depths. I wish that the rays of the Superconscious make way into your cave and light up your inner world forever.

INFINITE ANTIDOTE

You can exhale all your poison. You can cure yourself of its deadly effects—the poison of random thought, of random pulses in the nerves, of tensions uncalled for in the muscles, the poison left behind in the lungs by shallow breathing.

There is a physician inside who prescribes the internal antidotes. You yawn, and the lungs fill. You stretch, and the muscles relax. You sleep, and the brain takes shelter in the shade of the trees of negation. Your mind navigates a complex network of streams, channels and tributaries. Away from the toils of consciousness it views the festering swamps, the tropical woodlands, the fuming volcanoes of dreams. These are but imperfect antidotes, their effects lasting only a few, fleeting hours. Then you seek a deeper peace.

Your meditation is the herbal essence of Infinity. It is a serum that permeates your body, breath, brain. It is a drop of everlasting light. The light falls through a crevice, on a rock in the cave, and sets akindle the whole of your inner space.

Do take then, this day, an antidote for your daily doses of poison. Cheers to the immortalizing drink of eternal life and a forever lasting peace.

COME HOME TO YOUR SEAT OF MEDIATION

After wandering through the desert sands of the duties of the day, after bathing in the mirages of nightmares at night, come back home to the comforts of your spirit and rest. After scattering your gems to the world come back to your treasures to gather more. After searing your skin under scorching flames of passions, cravings, frustrations, return to your shelter for a healing balm. Once every twenty-four hours, do come home to your seat of meditation.[66] Come back home to rest.

All those swamps you waded through today have taken a toll on your mental body. The spirit is somewhat soiled, the splendour of the soul is somewhat dimmed. But here flows a sacred Jordan, the Mother Ganges.[67] From the mountain of your forehead a clear stream runs into the secret cave. Breathe deeply. Take a dip and bathe all the impurities away. Once more strengthened, venture out through the gates of your cognitive senses to hunt the experiences in the woods of the world. Travel, indeed, far and wide. But once each day, do come back to your seat of meditation, to the true home of your mind.

DANCE TO THE COSMIC TUNE

Driftwood floats at the mercy of every little ripple. A ship, expertly navigated, withstands mountainous waves. Little irritations and small emotions are for driftwood, not for the ships that free will navigates.

If you must be of earth, be the whole planet and not a tiny speck of dust. Be not a spark, but a conflagration; not a pool, but an ocean. If your self is little, a thousand sorrows a day will drown your specks of dust, a thousand little storms will extinguish your flame.

Let your meditation help you grow, help you know your vast, expansive Self, so that neither little sorrows make you weep nor small joys make you dance. Let your mind dance, indeed, but to the Cosmic Tune. Why is your meditation troubled by the small ripples of things of limited consequence when a still mind in meditation will bring you the Infinite?

If you must deal with problems this day, I wish you truly great problems, so you may find great solutions from the ocean of your expansive Self. I wish you an undisturbed mind, balance and equanimity.

LIFE FORCE

An ant's body is the size of a sesame seed, but permeated by life-force it exhibits amazing strength for its size. Imagine, then, the strength of the life-force that permeates the entire universe with all its outstretched stars and galaxies.

Imagine, now, blood cells in your body debating whether such a being as man exists and what the nature of man's life and consciousness might be. Feeble like the efforts of a single blood cell are one person's thoughts trying to comprehend the reality of life-force permeating the universe.

If you look inwards, in your meditation, you will find that the same life-force which flows through the ant, blood cell, the atom and the Sun,[68] is you. In the highest reality, all is you. In this knowledge of your own nature, a wave of peace washes you, a majestic wave of peace washes over you and fills your soul.

GIVE A MEDITATIVE LOVE OFFERING TO YOUR SOUL

It is never your ego's wish to go in search of intangibles, for the ego vulture feeds on the carrion of craving. But your wisdom is homesick for the inward-opening cave where the gold of intangibles and the gems of formless light wait for your spiritual rays to discover them.

However much you hunt for wolves of passion, the deer of desire; however often you comb the forests full of unde-fined hungers, at the end of the day your mind must go back home. Close down the portals of the senses, pull down the shades of your eyes and rest within.

Why do you not hear daily how your soul cries for your soul's love? Close all your doors and, in the most private cell of the monastery of your body, deep beyond the corridors of the brain,[69] give a meditative silence as your love offering to your soul.

MARRIAGE OF SHAKTI AND SHIVA

PILLAR OF LIGHT

You seem a little jumpy today, breath. Eyes, you are like straw tossed on a flood. Fingers, you are blades of grass in a storm. My beloved body, why are you blown like a leaf in the wind? Ah, mind, my familiar mind, you amaze me: how you squander all that energy, how you shun all that love, how you close the inward floodgates, how you sporadically spill into the reservoir outside you. You are like a mirage in the desert.

But I think it is time we had a conference. Come brethren, let us form a circle around a pinpoint of celestial light. Settle down on this sacred seat of meditation, draw yourself to yourself. Each of you, my body, breath and mind, let us be in harmony and worship together the pillar of light[70] that reaches up through the spine and further to the heights of heaven.

The sun shines from one side of this pillar, the moon from the other. They circle around it day and night, borrowing their light from its heavenly splendor. When all others sleep, he, in whose light the sun and the moon share, remains awake sending out the rays of wakefulness.

Brother breath, settle down. My body, go still. What is this, twitching fingers? Tongue, cease this twitter. Echos of my mind now subside. Here enters stillness, the beginning of silence. Purity now shares this dwelling with us.

I wish you this day a glimpse of the cosmic pillar of light.

SHAKTI

Lonely soul, have you met the charming woman[71] who shares your chamber? Lonely soul, she is beyond description. Take all the mountains of the world for ink and dissolve them in the inkpot ocean. Of a branch from the tree in paradise, shape a pen and make of this earth with its many layers the writing pad. If Sophia (Sarasvati[72]) herself writes from eternity to eternity, she will not come to an end of the descriptions of the charms of the woman who shares your chamber,[73] lonely soul.

All the sparks that fly in you: will, knowledge, action,[74] emotion, experience, percept, concept, love, light and truth, are specks of dust on that woman's feet. As she returns from her cosmic journeys, she returns for love of you.

The Lord gathers that dust from her feet, throws it into empty space and lo, the myriad suns and stars become as satellites of earth, like so many musical notes.[75] Have you counted the shades of color of the rays that emanate from a toenail of her left foot?[76] She wiggles her toe and a tiny ray, you, returns to rest at her foot. Her music calls and you meditate. When will you see her face, lonely soul?

I wish you this day a glimpse of the light in this inner woman's eyes. I wish for you a baptismal immersion in a wave of beauty of your own fulfilled Self.

EARTH PRISM

He is the dancer in the theatre of space,[77] where galaxies are toe steps in his intricate movement. She, the prima donna of the Universe's opera, boasts planets for her drums and milky ways for her harps. But my offerings are only the patter of my childlike feet, often out of step and a rattle in my throat, which I call "song."

On that artist's easel there are a million infras and ultras of color, the harmony of shades in a canyon forty thousand feet below the sea, the jeweled rays of a fire burning forty thousand planets away. But I can say that grass is green and the sky is blue, and I mistake myself for a connoisseur of art.

I have lit a candle to see the sun and tried to quench the ocean's thirst by pouring on its beach a handful of its own water. On a roaming musk deer I have sprinkled synthetic perfume. i have added sparks from my crude flint to the cosmic conflagration for which all the worlds are kindling at the end of an aeon,[78] and I think I have made an offering of worship.[79]

O, teach me this day that I am my mother's ovum, my father's seed, and the touch of a ray from an everlasting Sun. All of my heart in worship, all of my art in worship are but a tiny prism floating alone somewhere in infinite space and catching just one ray of Sun.

VEIL OF IMPURITIES

Your impurities, Self
    are the proof of your purity.
Sunlight in the evening,
    blue of sky,
    grey of patchy clouds,
    white silk of rays,
    green trees on lakeshore,
    a silver-dot star faintly appearing--
    the silver of moon in a corner,
    strands of reflexions in waters stretching far.
Skim from the waters
    the silver silvers, pinks, golds, greens,
    strands of multicoloured reflexion.
Weave of them a veil to wear
    as a lining inside your skull.
That veil reflects in the crystal of your mind.
See the Self reflect in it too.
Is the reflection of your face in the mirror
    adorned with the reflection of the veil?
    Or are you adorned, Self?
A lump of clay
however much you polish it,
surround it with silk
    or lights of many colours,
takes on nothing, reflects nothing.
Pure crystal becomes red
    in the presence of red light;
    false identities
    taken on by the sensitive.
Purer the crystal,
better the reflection.
Your impurities, Self,
are the proof of your purity.

WATER OF LIFE

Icicles, beautiful, of many sizes and shapes. An infinite number of snowflakes, each a sapphire of individual cut, prepared by an invisible master hand. The beauty of each, very personal, adorns the earth. But when the sunlight strikes, when the icicles and the sapphires begin to meditate on their own true nature, knowing finally, that their true Self is the crystal-pure water of life, the dark winter is over.

Earrings, bangles, coins in a mint, meditate on their origin and know that they are the gold of the deepest mine, and the glitter of them all is a tiny flame in the heart of the Sun. The rivulets meditate and flow to the rivers. As the meditation of the rivers grows, they rush to the ocean. In a mother's womb, too, the light of stars becomes flesh and your eyes are born. Brother icicle, my pure sister sapphire, fellow friend from the same mint, Lady River[80] undulating, laying parallel to me, let me whisper a cosmic secret to you tonight: "You and I are a multiple fetus with one life, of the same mother coursing through us in the Golden Womb of meditation."

I wish us this day a melting together of icicles and a light in the pinpoint core of pure sapphire, pure gold and peace.

POOL OF SILENCE

I stand quiet
   and dig a pool of silence
   around me
   filled with peace of waters,
   and I am an island.

I cast a tiniest thought
   or a word,
   a pebble,
   and the spirit of waters
   is awakened, thrilled.

The ripples come in circles
   larger, subtler,
   and kiss my shores,
   sending into my roots
   a wave of imagination,
   vision, creation;
   grass and shrubs and trees,
   nourished, shooting upward!

The ripples subside
   and I stand,
   an island,
   in my pool of silence.

RIVERS AND OCEANS

The rivers flow in many directions, each between its own two banks, each assuming its own name though the reality is only water.[81]   When the rivers empty themselves and become the ocean, their loss of ego-identity is their true gain. Only when you empty yourself into God's ocean as you meditate, will you know the nameless, boundless ocean-like spirit that you are.

Only when you divest yourself of all assumptions of false personality as you meditate, will you know the pure gold that you are.

A single field of cosmic energy has become heat, light and magnetism. That single field is all the atoms, stars, suns and the mass. So, too, only when you empty your mind of all else and fill it with the flowing power of the divine one as you meditate, will you know, in the vast cosmic field of consciousness, that wave of life, that certain intensity that you are. Be not a bubble on the surface of a river, but the expansive ocean of cosmic life and consciousness that swells in the heart.

This day I wish for you the ocean of the one to receive your rivers of the many.

DRINK THE FIERY ESSENCE OF WATER

Breathe in the mental essence of fire and the dark storms of your mind will be lit by a diamond bolt of lightning streaking across your spiritual skies. Drink the fiery essence of water.[82]

Rub sticks together till sparks jump forth,[83] and strike stones until the grass blazes beneath them. Know that it is the rubbing of breath against brain that melts the mind into a blazing pool in the fire of enlightenment.

Where will you find the wood for fuel? Where else but in the random thoughts of the active senses and the wasted effort of false cognition? Your actions and experiences reflect a myriad of past incarnations. Are they not fuel enough to burn in the fire of right knowledge and freedom?[84]

Uncover them from the wraps of the subconscious, like concealed letters of an illicit love, and make of them a bonfire for your eternal freedom. Then, breathe in the mental essence of that fire.

Drink the fiery essence of water, breathe in the mental essence of that fire, bathe in the pool of enlightenment and serve as a brilliant torch to all.

YOU ARE A FLAME

A flame looking at the objects around it does not admire their light. It does not wish to be luminous as they, for it gives them light through its own luminosity. You are like such a flame. Your consciousness is not created through objects you are conscious of. You become aware of yourself as pure consciousness when you meditate. If, for even one moment, you realize your Self-luminosity you are a blessed one.

You light a candle in the dark to look for your possessions, but do you also light a candle to find the midday sun? Your spirit in meditation is the fully ascendant sun. No other candles are needed to look at that deity of the inner space. Only a moth, but not a firefly, looks for a lamp, then why do you go begging for others' darkness?

I wish you this day just one minute of life when you know in your meditation that you are a Self-shining light casting away all darkness from around you.

THE ONENESS OF FIRE

You constantly ask: "What shall I do, friend? Fortune-teller, when shall I do it?" Your meditation answers by teaching you to ask: "What shall I be, God? When shall I be that?" You are the pure field of force that is Being. Your Being is like a white light, which remaining white, appears green through green glass. All time, all place, all modes, all your moods and endeavours are just variations of intensity in this field of Being.

Be, then, the pure field of Being. Let all waves arise and all tides flow but remain, first, the ocean. Become a flame, an ember, a spark, heat or light but remain, first, the fire.

Play the flute of your thoughts skillfully and I wish you this day the discovery of your nature as eternal Being from which the transience of becoming is created and into which it dissolves. I wish you a meditation of the oneness of fire in all its flames. I wish you a oneness with your Self.

THE CAVE OF THE HEART

The words that came into the minds and mouths of ancient prophets can come through you also. The cosmic vision Krishna gave to Arjuna[85] can come to your view. The wheels of law set into motion by Manu, Moses and the Buddha are wheels of your chariot too.

To say that the ancients alone could tread the holy ground is to deny the all-pervading holiness of the eternal spirit which pervades today as it did centuries ago. When you undertake a pilgrimage into the sacred land of your own heart and soul, the ground on which you stand will become holy and pure. Your meditation seat will become the mount from which the Christ speaks to centuries.

Whatever greatness was shown to earth by the eternal spirit through the sages of the past is also yours. Whatever they knew can also be revealed to you, for your forehead is the mountain on which the God of your meditation engraves his truth, and from the cave of your heart[86] flow the streams of inspiration as you meditate in pious, peaceful quiet.

SPACE OF CONSCIOUSNESS

Motionless in each motion is space.
Undivided in the divided is space.
Unchanging when all forms change is space.
Neither moving, nor unmoving,
    neither not moving and not unmoving,
    nor both moving and unmoving is space.
It goes nowhere, comes from nowhere,
    even when all come and go,
    and move to and fro--in space.
Finer, subtler, steadier than that space
    is your atman, the Self of life in
    chid-akasha, the space of consciousness.
When you make a jar, the space inside it is not born.
    Nor are you, the Self of life, born at the body's birth.
    And when the house that is your body is destroyed,
    you remain untouched,
    going neither to heaven nor to hell,
    nor yet staying right here.
    The vehicle moved, the space of consciousness
    neither moved nor stayed.
Childhood, youth and age happen to forms.
Those forms alone have names;
But you, pure space-like base of all existence,
    remain formless and unnamed.
When the waves of mind
    that arise like galaxies in the space of your skull
    subside in the pure field that is
    the space of consciousness,
    your expanse will far transcend the cosmos
    and the cosmos itself will be a speck
    in the space that is in your eye of consciousness.

GALACTIC SPANS

I

This yearning to hold galactic spans in my fists,
to dive into the pearly depths of oceans unfathomed,

This my stretching up to swing
    on the hanging vines of solar rays
    to clutch the heavenly heights
    of a starry foliage,
this my restless straining to break the chains of boundaries
spatial;

All this,
    searching for Unfound,
    wandering in Unexplored,
    uttering the Nameless,
    bedecking the Formless,

This hurling of stones
    into the pools of silence,
    of ignorant contentment....

II

This is the furl of my flying banner,
the emblem of my upraised standard,
the banner of life never subdued,
the standard of power never unsparked;
this my burning discontent
    is proof that I am life;

The piercing roar of my pulsing bloodstream,
the flooding ocean of my prana thunderous,
the wavy dance of my kundalini uncoiling,[87]
    ready to strike!

III

It is unto thee, Lord,
    that I drink not the waters of sleep,
    and I roam not
    in the shadows
    of the world of the dead,

    the sun-devoid dead,
    the dead,
    who dream not beyond their thoughts,
    who walk not beyond their todays and their forenoons,
    whose suns delve not deeper than the horizons of now,
    whose Venus sets
    and whose moon wanes,
        ere their heart-babes
        find the cry
        for suckling the breast
        of an eternal Hereafter.

THE GLORY OF SELF

See the beauty of the Self, the majesty of the Self.[88] The Self is the treasure in the adobe hut of your body. It is the magnetic current in a lump of black iron, the imploding energy in a molecule. Know the light of this Self.

Do not say: "I am alive." Say: "I am the life-force." Do not say: "I am conscious." Say: "I am the consciousness." For life is not a state, nor consciousness a process. The life and consciousness is one energy and that is you, the Self. The Self vibrates, so it magnetises. The Self shines, so it illuminates.

Sing, then, the song of the glory of Self: "I am Self. I have turned glass beads into gleaming, loving, glancing, crying and laughing eyes. I have made a piece of leather into an articulate tongue. What would have been dry kindling has become bones because I am present. Two gaping holes breathe my spirit and become nostrils. And when I am gone, this adobe hut crumbles while I, who am the gems of the whole universe, beautify a palace elsewhere."

Say, too, to your mind: "Brother mind, we have quite a journey together. I know you are mind, do you care to know me? I am the self-luminous Self."

This day I wish all luminosity to you.

SELF-KNOWING

Like your head, your Self is the source of all intelligence.[89]
Like your forehead, it is the tablet on which
      your fate is written.
Your Self soothes your brow when non-self knots it.
Like your eyes, it is the channel of Divine Light.
Like your nostrils, it is the breath of all breath.
When your intelligence traces its origins to the Self,
      it makes your fate,
         soothes your brow, becomes a channel of Divine Light
      of which your breaths become twin beams.
Know the Self; know thy Self.

It is from your Self that your speech proceeds and to which
      it returns in silence.
The enjoyment of all tastes has its origin in the Supreme
      Joy which is of the eternal Self.
Your shoulders carry your burdens because the strength
      that bears the Universe like a million Atlases
      flows in them from the Shakti strength of Self.
You are never weak, but always strong with the strength
      of those million Atlases.
Know the Self; know thy Self.

I wish this day that the peace of Self-knowing flow into you.
      In all your limbs, in all your life,
      Know the Self, know thy Self.

SAMADHI

She was the Void, neither being nor non-being.[90]
She moved not, nor was She unmoving.
The Mist that covered the eternity lay deep, unspeaking,
    unspoken.
A quest unto Herself, an answer unto none.

She was the terrible face of death in whom all,
    having been consumed, rested.
A night holding in Her womb the day-child awaiting the
    dawn of re-birth.

She was the all-embracing breath of deathlessness
    living in the heart of the Immortal.

A life unto death, a death unto life.
A light unto darkness, a darkness unto light.
A poise between the rhythmic steps of a dance was She.
The calm before the storm was She.

She was the bud concealing the flower that shall bloom
    into a thousand petals.
In her womb rested the golden egg, the cosmic Light, the
    expanse of the earth, the breath of the sky,
        and the wrath of thunder.

On Her waters floated the dreaming spirit of Names.
She, the formless one, conceived all forms.
She was the awakening that slept; she was the sleep
    that lay awake.

Who?
The mystery unrevealed, the vision undivined,
    the question unanswered,
        the answer unsought.

The being woven in the thread of non-being,
    the Zero measuring all,
    a chaos orderly, an order chaotic, a wonder deep,
    a search seeking Herself.

The Tao, the Word, the Shunya, and Brahman was She.
Nothing, Nowhere, Forever, Absolute, Not was She.
She was Dissolution, Creation, the chain for a link,
    the link for a chain, the sleeping Snake,
    the beads woven in thread,
    the thread measuring the beads,
    the rosary chanting her own hymns was She.

She was the Silence to Whose tune Shiva shall dance.[91]
She was the Voice to Whose music Shiva
    shall beat his drum.
The cosmic Consort of the Lord, She caressed Shiva's
    dreams!

And Shiva awoke.
Shiva the benevolent and terrible;
    all consuming, all creating.
Trident-armed, Shiva awoke.

BRAHMAN

Once before time
There was a point.
Imagine all billions of galaxies of time;
Multiply their light a billionfold;
the point held that virtue of light.
It was a living point.

The point resolved upon observing
all of its virtues, lives, lights.
The point grew and became a vortex,
willed vortex to an upward dimension,
became a line, the digit, one.

The one knew itself
all one, alone.
I am only one:
may I be more, many--
it reflected.
The reflection made a mirror, mind,
into which the one projected
and saw the second, other,
and knew, "We are now two."

It reached into the mirror
and drew two out.
The otherness made them fall flat,
one on top of other.

"I am your superior," said one.
"I am your foundation," said other.
"I am the original," said the first.
"Wrong, I saw you on the other side
of the mirror of my reflection
and came out to meet," said the second.
"I saw and drew you out of your prison of no,
to give you existence, you mere second," retorted one.

"I, the first, emerged from my reflection
so you would not be all alone when you came into being,"
said second, claiming to be first,
or was the first's claim wrong?
Maybe he was the mere second.
The conflict grew.
They sought a resolution,
a solution,
their union.
Third was born.

So it went
till three times three
met zero who enveloped them all
seeking to return them to one
and then to a point again.

The longing for unity among conflicting ones
continues through all numbers,
desirers absorb objects they seek,
nations wish to swallow nations,
premises with terms become conclusions,
planets fall into each other,
lovers long for the one in them
and again progeny appears.

Through amities and enmities
all try out paths of return
to the veiled single,
not knowing that in it all
the point alone broods,
reflects, observes,
becomes, unbecomes
all of the manifold many:
galaxies, wills, minds,
petals, factions, fractions,

restless in bloom, in droop,
centripetal, centrifugal,
entropies re-arranging
all ways in their systems.

Their "longings for union" are no longings
but cognitions of unity in point;
many rainbows in the drop.
At the word "longing"
living point unfolds many;
at the word "for"
two, that is wings, begin to fold.
At the word "union"
one enters the point
and all exclamations cease,
revelations silent.
At once after time
silence is the living point.

Not conclusion from premises,
not resolving yes versus no.
Not then, not there, nor That
but simply, and all enough:

Once before time,
At once after time,
I am, I am.
I am that I am.
I am the silent point.

Once before time
there was a point...
story retold,
circle, cycle, reflection,
again to silent point.

PART II

VALLEYS AND MOUNTAINS

I HAVE TURNED MY BACK TO YOU, MOTHER!

I have turned my back to you, Mother.[92]
Never again shall my feet cross this threshold
of your house.
If you want me back, you may run after me
barefoot and dustladen,
calling me endearing names and pleading your love,
but I will not return,
for, I have at last turned my back to you, Mother!

Long years was I an obedient son
and ran numerous errands for you faithfully,
with sore feet and a hungry stomach, often
in sun and rain,
through storms and floods,
braving many a hostile wilderness; but
when I was pursued by the urchins of the neighbourhood,
did you stretch your hand to protect me? No!
You stood in the doorway, smiling,
while they nearly tore me apart.
Then, no! I shall not be your son,
for, I have turned my back to you, Mother!

I am now out for a long and tortuous journey,
and I am so young and small,
but I have taken no provender from your house.
I will beg a morsel from a village farmer on the way
or apprentice myself in a craftsman's workshop.
I will walk hungry and in tatters
till I am out of this country
and make me a fortune in an alien land
far, far away.
Not a farthing will I send you,
nor a message,
for, I have turned my back to you, Mother!

Perhaps some nights I will lie alone
in that distant country
with tears of homesickness in my eyes.
Perhaps, no one knowing my sorrow,
I will want to come back to be held to your bosom—
but I will lie there,
on a hard floor,
in my aloneness,
and not pick up my bundle to start on a journey back,
till you have suffered all I go through,
till you have begged a morsel from a village farmer
on the way
or apprenticed yourself in a craftsman's workshop;
till you arrive there barefoot and dustladen,
even as I am now,
to fetch me back--
and even then,
when I see you approaching,
I shall not get up in haste to run for an embrace!
I will turn my back
to hear you calling me endearing names,
pleading your love,
promising your protection,
and perhaps you will come to hold my head
between your hands
to lift my face to wipe off the tears which I will be trying
to hide from you;
but for now,
and until then,
I have quarreled,
and turned my back to you, Mother!

DARK VALLEYS

To know a little of their ways and to lead them to the boundaries of my land, I visited here. "A moment's journey across the valleys and then I shall return to my throne," I assured myself and came this way. O, would that I had known of the soft silken nets concealed in every crevice of this land to snare an unwary traveler!

Lord of my own world am I, but a slave of slumber in this land. At times I hear the ecstatic music of my land as it floats across the valleys and the fragrance of familiar flowers is brought to me by the wind. My eyes are tear-filled as the memories of my majestic royalty haunt my nights. I choke back my tears and pretend that I have forgotten all my past and I let a smile flicker around my lips. O, happy are my captors each time I let my limbs be smeared with the dust of their land.

But my thoughts are secretly filled with the memories of the past, when my tears of compassion quenched the thirsts of many, when my robe was the solace to those who were wounded in battles and my love was an island where many a ship moored and many a mariner rested.

O, I long for one glimpse of the spire of my palace, one soothing touch of the dewdrops of my garden path, one sound from the birds that perch on the roofs of my temple.

They wish to please me and offer me their beads and pieces of broken shells, for that is all they have; little do they know of the rubies that deck the steps of my palace. They offer me seats in their council chambers, for little have they heard of my throne and my court. A grain of sand from the sea beach I show them in my hand and they say I have the pearls of the seven seas! The maidens of this land offer me the enticing candles of their virgin light, but little they guess of the joys that float on the pools of my inner chamber. They offer me their largest cups and tell me that I can drink of them for a life-time, but too small are these for me even to sup for an evening.

Little is their land and in small toy huts they live. Their happiest dreams are woven of the threads of death and the future of their hopes is my long-forgotten past. Their rest is weariness to me and their union my separation. Dust of the crooked path satisfies their hunger and never have they tasted of the ripe fruits that hang along the straight highways of my kingdom.

Toiling is their rest, noise their silence and a battle is their peace. Without hatred for many they cannot love one.

O, I cry day and night and my smiles are woven of sighs. The garment of my happiness covers the treasure of my sorrows, and though many may claim friendship none understand my tongue.

Just this once let me escape the captivating charms of their maidens: Just this once let this cup be taken away from me. Just this once let the strings of their nets be cut and let me ride over the waves of laughter and cross these dark valleys. Let this Winter be over. This once let the cup fall and be shattered and I shall never drink of it again. Just this once let me be free of this fetter and I shall never return.

I LOSE TOUCH WITH THEE

It is so long since the days of my freedom.
Scorching sun,
ocean that cannot quench the thirst,
is this world.
How far do I yet have to travel?

I see a glimpse of thee, smiling.
Others are being raised from the ground,
but to me thou sayest, "Be patient."
Then, other glitters pull me away,
and I hurry after them,
as a child runs from toy to toy.
Again, I lose touch with thee.

I DID NOT RECOGNIZE DEATH

Death came to garland me with her thoughts but,
drowned in the intoxicating music of life,
I did not recognize her footsteps.

To brighten and fill the void of my dark world,
disrepute came to sprinkle invaluable gems on my path,
but my unseeing mind let this boon pass unnoticed.

If I, a provenderless traveler, had withdrawn my soul
from exploring the beauty of the valleys
and had only felt the thorns hidden under the flower-beds
spread on my path, I would have been spared the inertia
that accrues upon reaching a destination.

The Lord of Destruction offered a drop of Divine poison[93]
unto me, but I, unfortunate soul,
rejected it as his impure scraps, or else I too
would have become one of the snakes
dancing to the rhythm of his cosmic drum.
At the arrival of that death for which I had kept a vigil,
alas, I blundered and retreated.

In a moment of weakness, I poured out of my heart
all the tears of my pathos. And the gleaming dew
of laughter usurped the throne of my sadness.

After singing this song, I will go to rest in the lap
of mother Sleep, so that no smile of mad fame may scorn
the sanctity of my disrepute, so that no view of the valley
may steal me from the touch of thorns when I descend
in my slumber from my erstwhile destination, so that,
at drinking the leavings of Rudra,[94] I may become
that snake whom no messenger of destiny may ever save
from the pain of being endlessly tossed
over the oceans of misfortune.

CRY ON, MY LOST SELF

Is not pathos the mother of all? Is not life's cradle formed in the pain of a mother's womb? Is not death a prelude to the soft baby's birth? Is not birth a preface in the book of death? Is it not that rest comes when all is drowned in the flood of dissolution?

O Glacier, white-robed sage, O pretense of purity, why shall I stop you from melting and dissolving in tears?

Cry on, my lost self, cry on!

There is an incessant flow of tears in the sky's eyes and his cries rain softly. There is a painful swelling in the ocean's heart and he sobs vehemently. The night hides her pure face in the veil of moonlight and sheds the tears of dewdrops silently.

O mountain, O link between earth and heaven, O empty shell of strength, how can I prevent you from weeping in the laps of vales and from sending out the rivers of tears?

Cry on, my infant self, cry on.

SONG OF INNOCENCE

God, I lost what you gave me.
I lost my innocence.
Would you grant it to me again?

That when they curse me, "idiot!"
I panic, wonder how they found out,
and renew diligent effort
to conceal that I am indeed a fool of God.
    O God, make me your fool again.

That when they expel me, "unclean!"
I am grateful they remind me
in what foul flesh-house I dwell,
whose every opening oozes,
and renew effort to walk out free.
    God, make me so pure again.

That when they reveal impassioned breast to me
I remember my own mother.
An infant to all women,
I call out 'Ma' and cling to suckle.
    Mother, make me your infant again.

God, I lost what you gave me;
guide me to where I might find it again.

SHOW ME A GLIMPSE OF THY FACE, BEAUTY

I see the newly wed bride of the sun riding
in a golden chariot of the morning and I see
a rivulet sobbing in a valley like a child lost
from her mother. I see the moon, shy of her own radiance.
She hides her face behind a veil of clouds.
And when a blossom is born in a forlorn jungle I behold
the dewdrop dancing to a tune of reeds and I see a vine by
the pool bursting open her leafy lids to watch
a ballet of swans.

They say I see thee when I see this all, but I wish to see
thee unclad, open in thyself, beauty. Reveal to me thy
secrets; show me a glimpse of thy face.

"I am in life, my son. Watch not a mere play of revolving
atoms arranged cunningly to imitate me."—I hear a voice
from nowhere. Is it thy voice from heaven?

I turn to look at life. I see that the cacophony
of a child's cry is sweet symphony to a mother's ears.
I see that the flesh, blood and bones of the loved ones are
adored by many as thy true presence. I see oceans
full of passion striking themselves on the rocks
of the shores of disappointments. These man-bodies,
these woman-bodies have frozen the stream that is our life,
but still, many seek thee there, in ever-dying forms.

Art thou in these frozen forms? I wish to see thee
unclad, open in thyself beauty. Reveal to me thy secrets;
show me a glimpse of thy face.

"Grasp not the handle but the naked razor blade.
Let all blood of pleasures and happiness trickle out

and let all consciousness fade and all eyes shut! Then, my
son, you will see me." —I hear the voice again.
Is it thy voice?

I desire no nectar from gods and I drink the poison
of suffering. My eyes are shut but I feel the glare of myriad
suns. I tear off my garments and cast off my skin.
Ah there! There is thy face--I cry out.
But why is there much confusion and such burning heat?

When I grasped the handles, when I lost myself
in the dead atoms of nature, when I loved
the mere outer wall of this imprisoned fountain of life--
was it thy reflection? Or, was it but a reflection of me?

No, I am not thou, my beauty. I am not thou. I shout
and an echo from the horizon repeats: "I am not thou!"
And I sob and wander aimlessly in the valleys
and mountains and my eyes are blinded with many glares.
I am hoarse and yet I cry: Reveal to me thy secrets, beauty;
show me a glimpse of thy face.

THE HIMALAYAS CALL!

From deep within the Himalayas call;
from deep afar the Himalayas call.
I fly and fly with wings aspan;
the white bearded peaks sublime
in the Himalayas of the heart
for their home, the heaven, pine;
glaciers of search for eternal oceans
cry out to Shiva:[95]
"Hold thou us, for we are thine."
From deep afar the Himalayas call!

The call, heard in a saddening whisper,
as in a dream a memory past
fleets on the flute of a moment deep,
like a flag, when upwards, passing half-mast
the whisper trips a melancholy mood
a tremble in the limbs
of pines, ferns, deodars,
that have millenniums up, heavenward stood,
from soul-embers all ashes jars.
From deep afar the Himalayas call!

The call comes louder, distances merge;
heaven, sky, earth, subdued all stand.
Winds now eager[96]
upwards, onwards,
a pilgrim's heart, on, cavewards urge:
"Listen my soul, listen in silence,
Master calls; do not rave.
Up, O king, why a slave?
Life immortal, why in a grave?
Thou, O Freedom's very own self,
why for bounded cages crave?"
From deep afar the Himalayas call!

"Awake, arise, the peak on high--
the solar orange of eternal renouncing,
the colour of colours in freedom bouncing,
the red flames of your own fire--
thouwards send reflecting,
lyre of heaven, harp of sun is tuning
songs of calling in wave on wave."
From deep afar the Himalayas call!

"You, O son of Aditi[97] cosmic,
Logos, Word of God thou, Everest,
how you call this petty death rest!"
"O Hanuman,[98] son of winds,
pick up this flaming mountain high;
hurt to death though thy soul lie,
here is balm from Himalaya's sky
with life and light to kindle thy breast."
"Ever thou onwards, ocean wave,
with flaming red to deck thy crest."
From deep afar the Himalayas call!

"Thou, O Garuda,[99] Vishnu's vehicle,
golden-winged thou, hie, thou, hie!
Kanchenjunga, Nada Devi,[100]
Vaikuntha's[101] milky way,
Sheshnag's[102] milky sea,
all this span your wings engulf;
who can put thee in cage of earth?
Who can tie its stones to thee?
Wake up, rise up, Lord awaits,
calls thee now to journey Hima-wards
thou, O Garuda, hie, thou, hie!"
From deep afar the Himalayas call!

"Thou, O Tandav's[103] drum of fury,
there on Kailash[104] Shivaji waits;

go thou, join the band of ganas;[105]
go thou, gloat in lake of Manas;[106]
off with snares, away with baits!"

"Parvati,[107] O daughter of Himavant,
born of rock, why steady not self?
Parvati, my river of wisdom,
Brahmaputra,[108] daughter of Brahman,[109]
why rush forth now salty seawards?
Why not love thy spouse, Mahadev?[110]
Find cave entrance, it grows late;
sitting timeless, meditate,
close your eyes, caress His dream,[111]
He will come then, thine to take!"

Thus it hammers, thus it calls
(my soul on sea-waves no more's tossed!),
urging, urging with power most,
the choir of stars from horizon-coast
calls ever louder, senses reel;
sky is filled with tandav drum-beats.
Off my soul, like skins from fruits,
unknown hands of heavenly host
unseen, untouched, my bodies peel.
From deep afar the Himalayas call!

"We wait for you on high Himalaya;
the bodies peeling in vision you feel,
the vision of future that is nigh.
Yourself will bodies cast
to steer your wings on even keel,
to reach the purity of snows eternal
where ends sorrow, where ends cry."
This they say and all is quiet
but in the forest of my heart
colours of freedoms new, now riot.

Wings I open, up I rise;
jewel within the heart of lotus,
just within my reach now lies,
shines in splendours undisguised.
From deep afar the Himalayas call!

The journey Hima-ward now begins:
across an aeon primeval past
where dwelt the spirit in mist enwombed,
away from all the alien dungeons
where for long I lay ill-doomed,
where the captors, the chains of senses,
me the Noumenon, in phenomena groomed,
across the sea of space and time
island-named and continent-formed,
I fly to Ganga of horizon prime
that joins the shore of dissolving dusk
with shore of creation-dawn sublime.
To depths of sea, I cast my "mine"
when far within the Himalayas call![112]

Milky Way's stream of light,
galactic Ganges--God's delight--
on the mountain peak of skull
becomes the Grace's waterfall,
enters head's majestic hall.
Wrapped in sky's cosmic shawl,
I am king of mountains tall.
Hear, world, my Himalayan call.
Hear, within, the Himalaya's call.

THE GROTTO

I live in a cave, a spacious grotto with many exits
of diverse contours,[113] many coloured beams of light
pouring in, radiating out—the thread of life
flowing to and fro.
My cave in a mountain, volcanic, shaking; quiet and restful
for long moments, and then again suddenly quaking.
This my cave looks out to roads and paths,
to valleys and other mountains,
to sailing clouds that lightning breaks into rows.
I sit and watch many a procession, shouting hilariously,
mourning silently, curious, halting to peep in at me,
or indifferent, passing while evenings diminish
or mornings grow.
Warm is the fire I have kindled and fed with life-fuel.
Ashen sleep I blow away.
Stirred awake, the embers glow, flickering footwork,
dancing shadows, grotesque paintings, darkness
mixed with outer lights and alien rainbows.
Afraid, I quit this fire, rushing to my river of depths,
silent waters flowing to quench
bursting, flaming thirst-volcanoes.
Safely tucked in the mountain's womb, cool, collected,
smiling, poised, I take a dip of withdrawal
in my subterranean river while abroad
the world's procession,
lost, wearied, whither-so-ever goes.

BELOVED INFINITE

Let me be a target of your compassionate eyes, infinite, my beloved infinite, or let my target be you and let me be an arrow sped from the bow of your cosmic sound called "Om." Let me ride the friendly breezes of the breaths on my way, and as an arrow becomes one with its target, so may I be one with you, oh my life, my higher life—infinite, my beloved infinite.

Love, you are my love. Joy, you are my joy. Whenever you are with me, I Am. When you are away, I cease to be. I am weak, lonely, defeated, depressed when I lose sight of you. A glimpse of you is my eternal victory, the victory that is yours, conscious one, the only conscious one of the universe —infinite, my beloved infinite.

I spend only brief moments with you, but the eternity that you pack into those moments is never enough for me. Yet, I turn away from your presence like a child leaping from his mother's lap to run to a shiny wrapper, not knowing why, never knowing why, and I lose the sight of you. My light, my solar light—infinite, my beloved infinite.

But now, for now and forever the bow is ready, the breeze is right, my target is before me. Let it be your hand that shoots. Let it be your sound that is the bow. Let this breeze be your breath. Let my target be you. Let this soul be the arrow, the soul that is your spark, well feathered, winged, free with your own freedom. I am you—infinite, my beloved infinite.

O, YOU ALL!

With all the slaves of the world it is true that when their master is present they are slaves and when the master is away they become their own little masters. But you and I, are we not unique? When you are present, I become a master and when you are away, I become a slave.

They say, if one drinks of water his thirst is quenched. But my senses open all their mouths and drink of worldly pastures, and the more they drink, the thirstier I become. When I close my doors and call back the herd of my senses, my thirst for those waters ceases too.

Then I sit by your shore and your roar fills me. When I plunge into your depths, your silence stills me. When I draw towards you, you turn your face away, and as I draw away from you, your string that tethers me pulls me. When I open my castle doors, alien things storm in, but as I close the doors of the senses I am made immortal by my higher Being, and if I empty myself, your love fills me.

O, you All, you who negate what is not and who posit all, when the world becomes my all, my great Self becomes small, but when you are the world's All in All, your cosmic quiet stills me.

MY BELOVED, MY LOVE

My Self, my Master, my God, my beloved, my love. I am tired of asking, begging, cajoling: "Give me bread, give water, nourish me, nurture me. Give me light, give me reality, give me immortality, infinity. Comfort me, give me solace, grant me a glimpse." I shall no longer ask, no longer beg for all these gems of your crown. Let me be the dust where you walk; let me be a fish where you wash your feet.[116] Next time make me not human, but make me a lily in the pond outside your palace, so that when you wake in the morning and come out for a stroll and your glances fall on me,[117] I may open my petals and exude to you a fragrance that is your own. Let me sing for you as a bird on the forest trail where you walk and let me fly to the sky when you, my sun, rise in the East. Let me be a leaf to fan you when you sit under the tree where I grow. Touch me and I will glow. Let me be a snake of lightning slithering where you will tread. Pick me up and wrap me around your powerful thunderbolt, holy ghost, my Master, to charge me, to charge me and forever chain me to your freedom, eternal freedom. Bind me to you, bind me to your freedom. Make me your slave to make me a master, or destroy me to make me immortal.

I thought I would not ask, but here I have asked again. Your will alone is henceforth my wish. Just make me dust where you walk. Make me a fish where you wash your feet. Let me be a bird to sing to you on a forest trail, a leaf on a tree where you sit, a slithering snake that you will kill,[118] a streak of lightning that you will wrap around your thunderbolt. Your will is my wish, and in asking this I have asked it all.

YOU PROMISED

You promised.
Three times you promised, making a cross
upon my heart center, you said:
"Hope never to die.
I shall raise you above death. I shall make you immortal."
I asked you: "Will I be enlightened,
incarnate this very time in this very house? Will I become
wise as the Buddha, full of light
with your eternity speaking through me?"
And sitting here, inside of me, not loudly
but with all the strength of your silence,
you promised to raise me above all darkness.

Then again I asked you: "Will I ever Be?
Will I ever be real?
Will I ever cease to be the consciousness of a mirage?
Will I ever be free of the snake in the rope?"114
I asked: "Where my shadow is, will there ever be light?"
And next to my shadow, you were my light,
and you promised
that I would be real.

The second time you promised
that I would be above darkness,
and the third time that I would be one with Christ,
that my soul would become Christlike, Buddha-wise.
Yes, and then you commanded I turn all my opinions
into your Truth. You asked my seeds to grow
into your flowers.
You asked my mirage to become your reservoir.

If I have failed to keep my side of the bargain,
I know at least that I have been true to my longings for you.
Is it not enough for the water in the clouds

that the desert sand calls for them?
So if not a Buddha, if not a Christ,
will you not make me at least a person who breathes
your breath and carries your light?
Will you not lead me from unreality to reality,
lead me from darkness to light,
lead me from death to immortality,[115] in this very life
as you promised;
my infinite Self, in my meditations,
as you promised?

SURRENDER

This day I shall say "namas"[119]—not mine! Of all things I have claimed, and of all my claims, of all my hopes and all my expectations, this day I shall declare, "not mine." Honor or ridicule, love or hate, attraction or aversion--all states that arise from out of me I shall abandon. To them I shall not react. Let me read this day the lesson of equanimity.

This day I shall cease to identify with my external conditions, successes, failures, sizes, shapes and forms. Let me affirm that I am a pure field of light, life, consciousness, ever-pure, ever-wise, ever-free. All my actions arise from my volition and not from situations that are around me, for I am who I am.

This day I have found within me my own ever-living soul of peace. This is my God, my teacher, my love.

This day, it is entirely up to my God to keep me or to abandon me, entirely up to my teacher in depths to teach me or to leave me ignorant, entirely up to my love to make me friends or to give me solitude, peace and light.

DIVINE LOVE

Prayer is the cry of longing for the joy of belonging; belonging is Meditation. In prayer you say: "I long for you for I love you." In Meditation: "You am I, I am You." Says Kabir:

When I am, you are not.
When you are, I cease to be.
This lane of Love, my friend, is very narrow,
Two cannot walk in it abreast.

Mansur, the Sufi of Iran, climbed the steps of a ladder to the gallows saying: "I go to the bed of my lover." He laughed and looked at the onlookers: "Come, lovers," he said, "join me. When you climb these steps to his palace, you are He as I am He."

Only in separation between the two can you cry, ask, beg, or plead; manifold desires arise when the folds of your mind wrap the manifold of the Universe. But, rather, pray truly, seal your lips, still your tongue, let no word-waves arise on the surface of your mind; and in the secret cave of your heart, let your higher Self raise the lower, and let the lower bow with clasped hands and declare to the higher, "To this day I was Thine and Thou wert mine, but now I am Thy own Self."[120]

MY GIFT

The mother gives her child a handful of grapes. A few, he crushes and paints her apron with, and one he tenderly puts between her lips.

I too have looked for something to give you, in gratitude, but whatever I pick as gift is first your own gift to me.[121] I find nothing that is mine, for even my "I" is but your own Self.

In this the Genesis of my Spirit, I, your innocent child, have gathered for you a handful of the jasmines you scattered in my courtyard.

Thinking that I have given, I look for your smile, but its love and joy I see playing on my own lips. Only then do I know you have accepted my gift.

SONGS OF FULFILLMENT

DANCE IN THE FLAMES OF THE SUN

Naked, I will dance in the flames of the sun,
and with my arms open to hug the whole universe I will
soar high in the skies. The blue ocean of sorrows
is no more for me—the orange of the light of dawn
will now welcome me to my own land.

I will deck my hair with all the stars, and the planets
will be my stepping stones across the narrow stream
of space. My bridal night has come, and there are
no more veils for me.

I will lie in the arms of my lover when I am weary
of my cosmic dance, and the twilight of the boundaries
of this universe softly whispers in my ears with a smile
that He awaits and the hour of union is nigh!

I am a maid of heavens, mortals. Farewell,
I have grown my wings again!

It was a stroke of fortune that you did not recognise me
when I fell amongst you and clothed my limbs in shame,
embodied myself in shame, with a body, hid myself
in shame, lest you tied me with the golden chains
of your desires.

Farewell, my hosts on earth; freed,
I have laid myself bare again.
Farewell mortals, I have grown my wings again!

FOREVER ASHINE

I reach upwards high on high;
my hands are raised;
my eyes are fixed to galaxies and suns;
beauty unveiled, no more shy.

My lilies bloom to touches of moonlight;
fresh is the zest and tang of heaven;
spring breezes fragrant in my nostrils;
sweet music of gandharvas, apsaras,[122] angels--
oh, joyous symphony! Earth is a lie.

Night is over and gloom no more;
doubts have vanished, all answers found;
knots of the heart all loosened through;[123]
white treasures of truth abound.

I shall lift the Govardhan of earth[124]
on little finger of left hand mine;
the heaven my head, the seas my feet--
the star of life, the candle of light
forever undimmed, forever ashine.

SPIRIT'S EASTER

At the end of a night of ignorance, your Self is the sun
   of light.
The morning waves over your mind from horizon
   to horizon,
   from head to toe surges an awakening.[125]

Through every breath of your life there comes a tide of bliss
from that spaceless, timeless other shore, where the
Enlightened ones frolic and swim in the sea of light. The
morning wave washes over your mind, then every pore of
your being proclaims—this is my day of enlightenment! The
sun has risen, the sun has risen indeed!

When your limbs no longer strain, when the infinite engulfs
the brain, when the soul no longer claims any form or even
a name, when the bliss of God is the only joy and worldly
pleasure is pain, and the fallen archangel is raised to the sev-
enth heaven again, then your body is host, your blood is
wine, your mind is a church and your consciousness knows
at the hour of ascension: Christ is risen, Christ is risen
indeed!

ENLIGHTENED BLISS

My breath is a whiff
of the spring flowers—
and not the sign
of a whirlpool's empty hollows.

My eyes are the rays
of the sun and the moon—
and not the glints
off the foot-trodden, broken shells.

My ears are the receptacles
of honey flowing day and night.
They are not the cups
of a deluding wine of passion.

My lips are the two banks
of the river of solace
and comfort to others—
and not the crater
of an empty volcano
pouring molten fire.

My life is a wick
burning without a flicker
before His image
in the cosmic temple—
It is not a lump of clay
crushed under a plough
and whipped about in a storm.

My mind is the silence of woods
in the light of the day—

and not the hooting drumbeat
of fear in the night.

My heart is a gift of life
that pours from the mother's breast—
it is not the stealthy throb
of a meteor's footsteps
rushing away
with the stolen wealth of stars.

My entire body is a harp,
with all its limbs, the strings,
tuned to the birdsong
of a morning-held sky-stream,
to health and vibrant feelings
of the universe.

It is not a prison.
Not a skeletal cage
to hide with darkness,
to chain with suppression
the ecstasy of enlightened bliss.

And since my hands are
strong enough to bless—
they are not so weak
as to wield a sword.

BE FREE! BE WHIMSICAL!

Be free! Be whimsical!

Dance on a precipice, laugh in a storm. In the middle of a murderous wrath, be still a moment and smile— then continue, angry.

Reach high and grab a bolt of lightning, as if to strike— but then, just illuminate. Be whimsical!

Gather with a hundred hands openly and give with a thousand in secret.[126] People play the game of goodness, hiding their evil. Change your rules today and appear evil when all within you is purity and love. Let them spit at you, for the joke is on them. Be whimsical!

Alone in a bath stand unclothed and bray like an ass or sing like a cuckoo—it's all your pleasure. Keep for the whole day that very solitude. Doff the gossamer silk of flesh to the blowing winds of your deep breath—then, dance alone as a vortex of light. If you want that freedom, then be whimsical!

Be a trickle to tickle a pebble or be a mighty ocean to wash a world. Make a mountain of your forehead or be minute to ride a butterfly. Change water into wine if you so wish. Play the games the Masters fancy—and only in that freedom, be whimsical!

BODHISATTVA[127]

Many have asked thee for the joy of a moment in the chambers of heavenly maidens and many have prayed for the privilege of sipping but a drop of the drink of immortals. They have given up their comforts, forsaken their gardens, and smeared their limbs with the ashes of penance today, hoping for a morrow of reclining under the shades of parijata[128] and of weaving a garment of dreaming moments.

But I, I shall not beg for those heavenly fruits when the day of my release comes!

I am saving up my joys so that I may carry a cofferful of them to scatter among those who have known none, and I am filling up my pouch with the healing breezes of ungiven love so that I may release them to soothe the wounds of those who endure the endless tortures of the nether world.

Send me not to heaven when I take leave of my leaking shelter of a hermit,[129] O, guardian of the scales of my action.[130] Write not many good deeds under my name in the book of memory, for I wish not to have my salty tears of compassion choked to death by the laughter of a sweet flower-dew of paradise. If you wish to grant me a favour, command thy messengers to send me to hell where I may change the cries of piercing agonies into happy smiles.[131]

SONGS OF SILENT WORSHIP

God, grant me this wish.
Grant me the high stature of a silent man.
May my footsteps be so soft no one hear,
but a perfume so gently waft into minds as I pass by
that a quarreling couple behind closed doors
suddenly go silent
and only wonder what strange peace,
from where, drifted into their hearts.
    O God, may it be so.

God grant me this wish.
No name be inscribed on this,
your unknown soldier's grave,
yet whoever hurries by feels an urge to halt
but never know that it was because
he had stopped at this mere dirt patch in the ground.
    O God, may it be so.

God, grant me this wish.
May I never interrupt my silence by a song,
but whoever brushes by me in a crowded bazar
feels a song of your praise arise in his heart and
helplessly pour out from his lips.
    O God, may it be so.

God, grant me this wish.
Like a secret love
may I never utter your name in the presence of those
who bear no love for you,
lest it hurt their un-matured feelings,
but my thought of you so jump like a star-spark across
that its echo fill the halls of their minds.
    O God, may it be so.

God, grant me this wish.
In my sleep I do not dream
but thereby those who lie near me
dream of you and
helplessly mutter your name in their sleep.
    O God, may it be so.

God grant me this wish.
May a million doubters shout their open-throated
challenges at me while I stand dumb, silent before them.
But thereby their questions be forever resolved
and their voices stilled within.
    O God, may it be so.

God, grant me this wish.
That I enroll as a private in some tyrant's army.
He gives an order to start a march of conquest.
I salute him, along with the rest of soldiers' company.
His glance accidentally falling on me,
a white dove flutters in his heart;
he calls a halt to the march
and sends a message of peace
to the weak neighbour land.
Never knowing me as the cause,
he disbands all his battalions.
I enroll in another tyrant's army.
    O God, may it be so.

God grant me this wish.
In tatters, I beg in the city streets,
and something comes over the rich and miserly.
They send cartloads of food to follow me
to give a feast to the hungry throng at the city gates
and then extend an open invitation to all the crowd
to eat at their homes for always from the next day.
    O God, may it be so.

God, grant me this wish.
May I become flesh in endless rebirths
only in the most difficult of centuries
and I, unknown,
ease the century into a time of comfort,
then ease myself out of my flesh to dwell in you till the
next difficult times.
    O God, may it be so.

God grant me this wish.
Whoever read or hear this
become so tranquil of spirit
that they seek the exact same wishes granted by you
and may they be fulfilled for them.
    O God, may it be so.

May it be so, God,
that hearing my prayers, these
you say only within my hearing
"May it be so, Son: I grant you your wish,"
"May it be so."
    O God, thus may it be so.

Epilogue

SILENCE OF THE SUN

The lights you see are diffuse, scattered; they strike a wall, reflect and cannot go beyond. But there is a light without measure in which there is neither beginning nor end,[132] neither now nor then, neither here nor elsewhere, but is all time, all place, now and forever. If a thousand suns would shine together in the sky in all their splendour,[133] such would be the light you see with eyes closed in meditation.

A fire has a few flames, a few sparks, a few embers and finally ashes. But there is a fire that has lit the sun, kindled the stars, a fire whose ember is earth When God decides to renounce the universe, prepares to leave the household of immanence to enter the monastery of transcendence, the innumerable earths, suns, stars, galaxies fall into that fire of final conflagration.[134] What remains is the ashes that God the ascetic then wears on Herself.[135]

When God again opens the doors of Her hermitage, the flame birds of all the universe rise from the egg that God shapes out of the ashes She wore.[136] That egg and those birds of fire you will see in the vast inner space behind the eyebrow with your eyes closed in meditation.

This day I wish you the revelation of a chariot of fire[137] drawn by the seven horses of light. I wish you entry into that world of light. Light.

FOOTNOTES

1. The *Vedas* are the book of wisdom, a collection of 20,000 hymns dated approximately 2,000-1,500 B.C., from which the rest of the literary and philosophical tradition of India has derived its inspiration.

2. Swami Rama Tirtha was a great philosopher and yogi who lectured and taught extensively in India and in the United States in the beginning of this century. His name is well-known to the students of Indian religious developments of modern times. A number of books including academic works and theses have been written on his life and philosophy.

3. The Golden Womb is an idea somewhat parallel to the Holy Ghost as the teacher and source of all inspired knowledge.

4. Read *Living With the Himalayan Masters* by Swami Rama, Published by Himalayan International Institute of Yoga Science & Philosophy, Honesdale, Pennsylvania, 1978.

5. Compare a well-known Sanskrit hymn. "He whose grace makes the dumb articulate, makes the lame climb a mountain, to that supremely joyful Lord, my homage."

6. Wherever in the mystic literature there occurs a description of a teacher going up a mountain it actually means the consciousness rising to the centers of wisdom inside the head or behind the forehead.

7. In Hindu mythology one may recognize a god by five marks. The god's feet do not touch the

ground. His eyes do not blink. There is no dust on the body, nor is there withering of the flowers in the garland worn. He will cast no shadows and his body is not solid but a configuration of energy.

8. Kalki, the future incarnation among the ten major Hindu incarnations of God

9. These lines explain the fact that some of the poems speak of the darkness and despair experienced by the aspirant rather than by the perfect being. Such verses could not represent the knowledge and feeling of the god incarnate.

10. The cave is a symbol for inner centers of consciousness. In the texts such phrases as, "in the cave," "in the cave of the heart," "in the heart" are often repeated. See *Katha Upanishad* I.2.12; I.3.1; *Mundaka Upanishad* II.1.10; *Shvetashvatara Upanishad* III.13, 20 and IV.17, 20; *Bhagavadgita* XVIII.61.

11. The aim of the Sankhya and Yoga philosophies is the total and permanent eradication of all pain. This, says the text *(Sankhya Karika* 1.2), cannot be accomplished through the fulfillment of desires. Also, *Laws of Manu* II.94.

12. Pure Consciousness *(Atman)* is the true Self, the unchanging, eternal Truth that is beyond the entire manifest world. *Atman* is the eternal Self which permeates the waking, dreaming, and deep sleep states and yet remains transcendent, above all mundane pains and pleasures. *Atman* is the individual Self which according to Vedanta philosophy is identical to the transcosmic Self, the absolute reality, Brahman. The yogi reaches his own inner Self in the highest stage of *samadhi* (enlightenment).

13. This refers to a part of the daily ritual of meditational worship, *sandhya*. The other elements of this poem, such as the celestial thoughts concerning the rivers at the time of the bath, and burning the evil man are all derived from the same form of worship. The *sandhya* is performed two or three times daily by the devout disciple of meditation.

14. This is literally true of the temples of India. The daily ritual includes the statement that: As many streams of water falling from the sky and flowing through many rivers all go finally to the sea, so the worship offered to all the deities reaches but one God.

15. Sarasvati in Hindu mythology is the deity of wisdom, inspiration, speech and music.

16. The original sentence was, "Do not let your love be a service only to your urges, but let it serve the harmony of Cosmic Truth." The editor has changed "urges" to "desire."

17. In the Yoga tradition, and in the culture of India, the purpose of marriage is to unite for life, in order to walk together towards union with God, by paying off karmic debts together. It is not a contract with each other but an offering to God.

18. *Laws of Manu* IV.160: "Know this briefly to be the definition of pain and pleasure: everything in which one is dependent is pain; everything in which one is independent is pleasure."

19. The true nature of inner consciousness is that of a witness and not of a participant in the modulations and interactions that go on in the material body and the world. See *Shvetashvatara Upanishad* VI.11.

20. Paraphrased from the *Aitareya Brahmana* VII.33.3.

21. "A wise man, though educated, should appear uneducated." *Mahabharata, Udyoga-parvan*, 42.38 (Gita Press Edition).

22. In the Indian tradition of aesthetics and poetics, the nine basic emotions are ascribed various colours, and laughter is considered white.

23. This poem was written on the occasion of Holi, the festival of colours that comes in the spring. On this day, all over the cities of India the barriers between castes, relationships and age groups are completely broken; people throw coloured powder on each other and soak passers-by with coloured water shot from syringes. All enmities must be forgotten and those who have been hostile to each other must meet and embrace.

24. From the teachings of Shantideva, an eighth century Buddhist saint.

25. Nathur Godse assassinated Mahatma Gandhi on January 30, 1948.

26. "The reality is one; the wise give it many names," *Rig Veda* I.164.

27. *Shvetashvatara Upanishad* VI.20: "When men will be able to wrap themselves with (empty) spaces like a piece of leather, only then will there be an end to sorrows without knowing the divine."

28. The horns of a rabbit, flowers of the sky, the natural son of a barren woman are all stock examples of permanent negation or impossibility in the Indian systems of philosophy.

29. *Katha Upanishad* I.2.10: "Whatever is here is there, what is there is here."

30. Compare *Katha Upanishad* I.2.20.

31. This is the practice of *smriti* in the Yoga, or *Sati-patthana* in the Buddhist tradition, mindfulness, which is taught systematically and methodically in all the schools of meditation.

32. See the *Laws of Manu* IV.138: "Let one speak truth. Speak pleasantly. Do not speak unpleasant truth. Do not speak pleasant untruth. This is the eternal law."

33. See *Yoga Sutras of Patanjali*, II.38: "When one has attained the *siddhi* of truth, his words unfailingly come true."

34. The original Sanskrit verse is, "Better to burn bright for a flash than to smoulder for long."

35. "When the *siddhi* of non-violence is attained, there is no violence in (the Yogi's) presence." *Yoga Sutras of Patanjali*, II.36.

36. "Knowing the entire world to be one with Sita and Rama, I join my hands and bow to the whole world," says Tulasi-dasa, sixteenth century saint, devotee and poet in the *Ramacaritamanasa*, Canto I, Doha 7g.

37 The common greeting of Asia is explained, in which clasped hands are brought to the heart and the head is bowed. It is the same as the Christian gesture of prayer.

38. This is addressed to those who are intolerant of the idea of a graven image.

39. Certain very special types of oval or round pebbles are used as symbols for worship in some Indian religious traditions. They are not images but symbols of the formless perfection of God.

40. For this reason the cow is referred to as mother, *go-mata*, throughout India.

41. It is believed that God may incarnate in any form, not necessarily a human one. There are many stories relating to such incarnations.

42. According to the Vedanta philosophy, God does not create the world but becomes the world by the transcendental reality manifesting from within itself the empirical reality.

43. This paragraph is a paraphrase from the well-known mystic, king, saint and poet of the Sanskrit language, Bhartrihari (circa Eighth Century A.D.), who wrote three centuries of verse. This is from the *Century on Vairagya*, verse 3.

44. These are various methods of concentration and meditation.

45. These four steps are prescribed both in the Yoga and Buddhist traditions for cultivating the habit of right thoughts.

46. The expirations and inspirations of your vital energy is *prana*. The word *prana* is composed of two words, *pra* and *na*. *Pra* means "first unit" and *na* means "energy." The first unit of energy is in its subtlest aspect in man; the universe is its expansion. Thus, there is no qualitative difference between man and universe. It is *prana* that feeds and sustains the mind and produces thoughts. It is linked to the mind, through mind, to will, through will to the individual atman and thus to the cosmic soul, and then to the trans-cosmic Brahman. All sensations, all thinking, feeling and knowing are possible only because of *prana*. Learning to still and control your breath *(pranayama)* is one of the primary meditative vehicles for realizing one's universal Self. The etymology of *prana* given here is according to the oral teachings of the yogis. The grammarians derive the word from *pra*, forth; and from the verb root *an* to breathe, to be vital, to be alive, same as found in words like anima, animal, animate.

47. Compare also The Five Books of Moses: Exodus III.14. "I am who I am," and "Before Abraham was, I am," from John 8.58 in the New Testament.

48. The center of consciousness between the eyebrows, called *ajna chakra*, is said to be the seat of wisdom and inspiration in the Yoga tradition.

49. The poem explains the meditational technique of concentration on breath as follows: concentrate on the flow of breath in your nostrils; exhale and inhale without a pause between the exhalation and inhalation. Whenever a pause occurs, be especially watchful because then many distracting thoughts can enter the mind.

50. Sacrifice of the seven priests, the abandonment of lesser ego to the expansion of energy through the seven centers of consciousness.

51. This poem is a paraphrase of *Yajur Veda* 34.6. "As a charioteer leads his horses, holding the reins fast, so does the mind lead all men; may this my mind be filled with beautiful thoughts."

52. Compare *Katha Upanishad* I.3.3-6. "Know the power of the self to be the owner of the chariot; know the body to be as the chariot, the intelligence to be the driver, and mind to be the reins, and the senses as the horses." "The senses are like the uncontrolled horses of a charioteer for one who is devoid of wisdom and has an untrained mind. But for one who is endowed with wisdom, and has a controlled and pure mind, the senses are like the good horses of the charioteer."

53. Compare the *Bhagavadgita* VI.19.

54. *Japa* is repetition of one's *mantra* given for meditation by a meditation guide. *Mantra* is a combination of syllables, or words, representing various psychic and spiritual energies. Through constant practice of *japa* within meditation and in active life, the power of the *mantra's* spiritual energies are released into one's inner personal constituents.

55. A question in Sankhya philosophy is: If self is ever-pure, ever-wise and ever-free, what causes it to have the illusion of impurity? The answer is that the mind, which is the finest form of material energy, serves as a mirror. When the mirror is unclean, the self, seeing its own image reflected in it, considers its own face to be impure.

56. This poem can be used as a mental preparation for meditation.

57. Compare *Katha Upanishad* II.3.1, and *Bhagavadgita* XV.1.2.

58. In one of the most well-known images of Krishna, he is playing the flute. All the cowherds and cowherdesses and dwellers of the nearby villages are charmed by his music and come flocking. It is said he had 16,000 female consorts. These represent the energy currents in the human personality. The word "Krishna" means "he who draws and attracts."

59. This is based on an initiatory experience.

60. Refers to one of the very first meditational exercises. The word "*so-ham*" reversed, "*hamso*" is the sun, the swan, the breath, or the solar swan of the breath. For details see author's book *Mantra and Meditation* (Himalayan Publishers).

61. See note 54.

62. In the practice of Nada Yoga, the Yoga of sound, the initiate hears many different types of sounds in his meditation.

63. In divine consciousness, a few incarnations take a very brief period of time.

64. This refers to the meditative breath as explained in note 49.

65. Compare *Kena Upanishad* IV.29. The lightning-like flash of wisdom is often described in mystic literature, especially in the Tibetan literature where the experience is called *vajra* or *dorje*, the thunderbolt.

66. An initiate maintains a fixed place and a definite time for meditation in his daily schedule.

67. It is a part of the daily worship rituals to visualize an internal path—-the rivers of peace and energy flowing from inside the head to all the extremities. Baptismal immersions and sacred baths in the rivers both in the Christian and Hindu traditions are external symbols of the inner steps for purification.

68. "He who shines in the sun, I am." *Yajur Veda* 40.17.

69. Yoga science regards the brain as a physical vehicle of only a small part of the mind.

70. The pillar of light is a well-known mystic vision. In the Yoga tradition, it is the force of universal life and consciousness flowing through the spine. More specifically in Kundalini Yoga it is the vehicle of the marriage of *Shakti* (the female creative force of universal life) and *Shiva* (the male aspect of Consciousness itself), which leads to *samadhi*. The phallic symbol of Shiva is known as *jyotirlinga*, the mark or pillar of light. The pillar of light is also know as Meru, the central mountain of the earth, behind which the sun rises and sets. The left nasal breath is known as lunar and the right nasal breath as solar. Hindu mythology also speaks of a pillar of light that Brahma, the creator, and Vishnu, the preserver, saw in the beginning of creation. One went downwards and the other went upwards to find its beginning and end. They explored for an eternity and came back to confirm that it was endless.

71. The charming woman referred to here is Shri or Shakti, the divine feminine force of the

entire universe. The poem speaks of the initiatory experience in which the entire universe and consciousness are seen as vibrations of divine energy. The greatest text on the subject is *Saundarya-lahari*, "The Wave of Beauty," by Shankaracharya (eighth century A.D.), the epitome of the Tantric tradition.

72. See note 15.

73. This is a paraphrase of the *Shiva-Mahimna* hymn, stanza 32.

74. Will, knowledge and action comprise the three-fold Shakti, power, or potentia of the Supreme.

75. *Saundarya-lahari*, verse 2.

76. There are many passages in the texts referring to the light emanating from the deity's toe-nail.

77. Shiva the cosmic dancer. The prima donna is Shakti.

78. In the Indian cosmology the universe goes through infinite cycles of creation and dissolution, each lasting many billions of human years. At the end of a cycle all the galaxies and the worlds, of which there might be as.many as the hairs on the body of God, fall into each other in a cosmic conflagration.

79. The simplest form of Hindu worship on an altar consists of five offerings: fragrant powder representing the earth elements and the first chakra (the center of consciousness where *kundalini* lies dormant and from which she rises through the other centers), water or milk representing all waters of the universe and the second chakra, the flame of a candle representing all fires of the universe and the third chakra, incense representing all air and the fourth chakra, and flowers representing all space and the fifth chakra.

80. Rivers are feminine because of their flowing, graceful quality and because waters are the symbol of motherhood.

81. Compare: *Chandogya Upanishad*, VI.10.1-3, *Mundaka Upanishad*, III.2.8, *Brihadaranyaka Upanishad*, III.8.9, and *Bhagavadgita*, XI.28.

82. In Vedic and Yoga mysticism, fire is born of water. The fire center awakens after the water center. Even now, some holy places of water for the immersion of pilgrims are referred to as *agni-kunda*, fire pools.

83. For the Vedic fire sacrifices, this was the way to produce fire. For the mystic significance as explained in this poem, see *Rig Veda* III.29.2, *Katha Upanishad* II.1.8, and *Shvetashvatara Upanishad* I.14.

84. This is from the *Bhagavadgita* IV.37.

85. See the *Bhagavadgita* XI.

86. See note 10.

87. Kundalini Shakti is represented as a resting snake at the base of the spine.

88. This poem illustrates only a little of the content of many hundreds of hymns in Sanskrit literature on the glory of the Self.

89. Compare this poem with *Rig Veda* II.39.

90. Based on the creation hymn, *Rig Veda* X.129.

91. Compare with poems entitled Shakti and Earth Prism.

92. The mother is Shakti. In order for one to reach God, one must pass through the lowest depths of despair to the point where even despair is abandoned.

93. In the *Puranas* the *devas* and the *asuras*, the divine and the demonic beings, churn the milky ocean to find *amrita*. One of these objects was the cosmic poison called *kala-kuta* literally, "the secret essence of time." The *kala-kuta* began to spread throughout the whole universe, and the gods were disturbed to see all the living beings choking to death yet found themselves helpless to stop its spread. They all came to Shiva who was sitting in *samadhi*, his deep eternal meditation. They awakened him by singing hymns of praise and finally he agreed to gather and swallow the poison in order to save the universe. A hymn in the *Rig Veda*, X.136.7, says: "The ascetic too shared with Shiva that poison cup."

94. This refers to Shiva in his terrible aspect as the dissolver of the universe.

95. Shiva's traditional abode is said to be in the Himalayas.

96. This refers to the *pranas*, the subtle forces of vitality generated through the practices of breath control.

97. Aditi, the mother of solar deities, is the Vedic goddess representing the principle of cosmic unity, literally the force of undividedness, indivisibility.

98. Hanuman, the well-known monkey god, is said to be the son of the wind god. Many miraculous powers are attributed to him. He swallowed the sun as an infant, whereupon he was given a curse that he would forget all his powers until someone reminded him. Such is that state of the pure soul that attributes to itself various impurities. Hanuman is also said to have picked up a mountain peak from the Himalayas and taken it to the battlefield of Ceylon so that the herbs from this peak could be used to revive Lakshmana, the brother of Rama, who is a well-known God-incarnation.

99. Garuda is the mythical bird that Vishnu, God the preserver, rides. This represents, mystically, the golden-winged free soul. In the sacraments of purification during pregnancy the father addresses the unborn child, "You are a beautifully-winged bird."

100. These are well-known peaks in the Himalayas.

101. Vishnu's heaven.

102. Shesha-naga is the coiled up serpent of eternity or the residue of matter after the cyclical dissolution. Vishnu sleeps on this coiled up serpent of eternity in a milky ocean.

103. Tandava is the cosmic dance of Shiva.

104. This peak in Tibet is said to be the abode of Shiva.

105. The attendants of Shiva.

106. The mind, also a lake behind Mount Kailasha in Tibet.

107. The feminine consort of Shiva is daughter of the personified mountain, Himalaya.

155

108. This well-known river flows from the Himalayas.

109. "Brahman" is a neuter noun denoting the God-force as unpersonified, unqualified, Supreme.

110. The great god, Shiva.

111. Parvati was determined to wed Shiva in this cycle of creation as she had been his wife in the previous ones. She chose the life of meditation since she could not otherwise arouse him from his own eternal meditation. When her own ascetic pursuits reached the pinnacle of their strength, Shiva broke his meditations and appeared before her.

112. This poem of longing up to here was written in 1962, with a note, "the poem will be completed when the journey to the Himalayas has begun." The next stanza was written, completing the poem, in 1971 after I was given initiation into solar science by the walking Himalaya, my Master. The stanza describes the initiation.

113. The cave here is the personality, and the exits are the senses.

114. According to the Vedanta philosophy, there are three levels of reality. In the transcendental reality, both the snake and the rope are Brahman, the Supreme being. On the empirical level of reality, the snake is a snake, and the rope is a rope. In an illusion a rope may be mistaken for a snake and a snake for a rope. The empirical reality is illusory so far as a man of perfect realization is concerned. We view this world as real because of our illusions, much as a person sees a snake in a rope in a dark room, or in a desert a mirage may appear to be a reservoir.

115. This is quoted from *Brihadaranyaka Upanishad* 1.3.28.

116. This is paraphrased from a devotional poem addressed to Krishna by a Bhakta poet, sixteenth Century A.D., in the Braj dialect of North India.

117. According to *Sukhavati-vyuha*, a Mahayana Buddhist text, some blessed souls are born in the Sukhavati heaven as lilies in a pond and when Buddha comes out for his morning stroll his gracious glances fall on them.

118. According to the Indian theology, one of the relationships one may establish with God is that of an enemy. A total enemy of God will be completely preoccupied with the thought of God and must therefore draw God's attention. One who may provoke God enough to die at his hand will definitely go to God's own abode. One example of drawing God's attention through one-pointed enmity is that of the Roman official Saul who became St. Paul.

119. *Namas*, which means not mine, also implies: it is yours Lord. It is the way of nonattachment and sacrifice where all is seen as being and belonging to Brahman.

120. Venerable Swami Rama in various sermons and teachings.

121. "Your own gift I offer to you as a gift , my Lord." From the daily ritual prayers of India.

122. *Gandharvas* and *apsaras* are, respectively, male and female singers and dancers, the ideal of physical beauty often known to visit the earth. The English word "fairy" derives from *apsaras*. Shakespeare, in *A Midsummer Night's Dream* (II.1,2), speaks of the fairies' connections with India.

123. Compare *Mundaka Upanishad* II.2.8, "The knot of the heart is burst all doubts vanish, all karmas diminish when that Supreme one is seen."

124. Krishna is known to have lifted the mountain Govardhana on the little finger of his hand.

125. This is a meditational experience from certain practices of breath awareness.

126. *Atharva Veda* III.24.5.

127. The *bodhisattva* in Buddhism represents the principle of compassion. The *bodhisattva* is one who has achieved the realization of immortality yet voluntarily participates in the sorrows of the world.

128. *Parijata* is the all-shading, wish-fulfilling tree in paradise.

129. This leaking shelter is the body and the hermit is the soul.

130. The inner arbiter who witnesses all our right or wrong acts.

131. This poem is based on the story of the King Rantideva, in the religio-philosophical epics of India called *Puranas*. When King Rantideva was being taken to heaven after leading a very virtuous life, he had to pass by hell because of some small infraction committed as a king. The breeze touching his body brought a very soothing feeling to the inhabitants of hell who cried out for him to stay. Out of the compassion of his heart, he told the heavenly messengers that he would rather stay in hell than go to heaven. When these messengers insisted that he was bound to go to heaven in accordance with the law of *karma*, he donated all his good *karma* to the inhabitants of hell to reduce their agonies.

132. Based on initiatory experiences.

133. *Bhagavadgita* XI.12, XV.12.

134. This again refers to the cycles of creation and dissolution.

135. Ashes from sacred fires are worn on various parts of the body by devout worshippers. The ashes may also be given by a holy man as a gesture of grace. The ritual formula for the daily application of the ashes reads, "Fire is ashes, the wind is ashes, the water is ashes, the ground is ashes, the space is ashes. All this world is ashes. The eyes, the mind, the senses are all ashes." Compare the tradition of Ash Wednesday.

136. The Sanskrit word for the universe is *brahmanda*, the Brahman's egg.

137. The *Rig Veda*, X.63.10, says that the deities ride the chariots of light. Compare the chariot of fire, 2 Kings II.11-12.

FULL CIRCLE

FULL CIRCLE publishes books on inspirational subjects, religion, philosophy, and natural health. The objective is to help make an attitudinal shift towards a more peaceful, loving, non-combative, non-threatening, compassionate and healing world.

FULL CIRCLE continues its commitment towards creating a peaceful and harmonious world and towards rekindling the joyous, divine nature of the human spirit.

Our fine books are available at all leading bookstores across the country.

FULL CIRCLE PUBLISHING

Registered Office
18-19, Dilshad Garden, G.T. Road, Delhi 110 095
Tel: 228 2467, 229 7792 • Fax: 228 2332

Editorial Office
J-40, Jorbagh Lane, New Delhi 110 003.
Tel : 461 5138, 462 0063 Fax: 464 5795

Bookstore
5B, Khan Market, New Delhi 110 003
Tel: 465 5641, 465 5642
email: fullcircle@vsnl.com

PIGS EAT WOLVES
Going into partnership with your dark side
by CHARLES BATES

A RADICAL FAIRY TALE FOR ADULTS

Have you ever thought that the Three Little Pigs was a story of your own transformation? Think about it. What if you were the little pigs — all three of them. Who is your wolf? What does it say about your own past, present, and future?

Pigs Eat Wolves will evoke memories of your childhood and show you what to do with the fears you brought to adulthood.

The book challenges us to accept, as part of our being, those characteristics which we would like to see only in others.

Join the
WORLD
WISDOM BOOK CLUB

*Get the best of world literature
in the comfort of your home at
fabulous discounts!*

Benefits of the Book Club

Wherever in the world you are, you can receive the best of books at your doorstep.

- Receive FABULOUS DISCOUNTS by mail or at the FULL CIRCLE Store in Delhi.
- Receive Exclusive Invitations to attend events being organized by FULL CIRCLE.
- Receive a FREE copy of the club newsletter — The World Wisdom Review — every month.
- Get UPTO 25% OFF.

Join Now!

Its simple. Just fill in the coupon overleaf and mail it to us at the address below:

FULL CIRCLE PUBLISHING

J-40, JORBAGH LANE, NEW DELHI - 110 003
TEL. : 462 0063, 461 5138 • FAX: 464 5795